Prais

"A generous account of transformation that reminds us we're sharing a collective experience of awakening on this planet."

—LISA RENEE, founder of Energetic Synthesis

"*Star Sister* resounds with integrity, honesty, and fearlessness. And it will inspire similar qualities in its readers. This is an exceptional story."

—MARK SINGLETON, author of *Yoga Body: The Origins of Modern Posture Practice*

"This strange story of a woman lost and suffering in the empty wastes of affluent suburbia shows just how important it may be that we rediscover our connection to place: Stella's healing comes through reconnecting with the magical-realist world of her Andean roots, where she is able at last to become herself. A truly liberating tale."

—HENRY SHUKMAN, author of *The Lost City* and *In Dr. No's Garden*

"As a journalist, I worship facts, research, things that can be seen, not mystical musings. But the odyssey that Stella Osorojos relates is strong and pure, a delight to share, and compelling enough to open a skeptic's heart."

—AIMEE LEE BALL, journalist and coauthor of *No Time to Die*

"Stella's funny, educational, and deeply wise memoir is a roadmap for the pathless path, as well as an invitation to join her in living an awakened life. A real page-turner."

—CYNTHIA JURS, Buddhist teacher and founder of Open Way Sangha

STAR SISTER

How I Changed My Name,
Grew Wings, and Learned
to Trust Intuition

Stella
Osorojos

Evolver Editions
Berkeley, California

Published by Evolver Editions

Evolver Editions' publications
are distributed by
North Atlantic Books
P.O. Box 12327
Berkeley, California 94712

Cover photo by Genevieve Russell
Art direction and cover design by
michaelrobinsonnyc.com
Book design by Suzanne Albertson

Printed in the United States of America

Star Sister: How I Changed My Name, Grew Wings, and Learned to Trust Intuition is sponsored by the Society for the Study of Native Arts and Sciences, a nonprofit educational corporation whose goals are to develop an educational and cross-cultural perspective linking various scientific, social, and artistic fields; to nurture a holistic view of arts, sciences, humanities, and healing; and to publish and distribute literature on the relationship of mind, body, and nature.

North Atlantic Books' publications are available through most bookstores. For further information, visit our website at www.northatlanticbooks.com or call 800-733-3000.

Library of Congress Cataloging-in-Publication Data

Osorojos, Stella, 1971–
Star sister : how I changed my name, grew wings, and learned to trust intuition / by Stella Osorojos.
    p. cm.
  ISBN 978-1-58394-374-8
1. Osorojos, Stella, 1971– 2. Spiritual biography. I. Title.
  BL73.O86A3 2011
  204.092—dc23
  [B]   2011041217

1 2 3 4 5 6 7 8 9 MALLOY 16 15 14 13 12
Printed on recycled paper

For Aaron, my greatest teacher.
For Pamela, my hero.

Acknowledgments

Thanks to Aaron, for unending support and love. To my parents, for their generosity and understanding. To Cynthia Adolfson, for encouragement at the exact right moment. To Amely Greeven, Clare Dunne, and Dana Schwarz, LAc, for helpful early reads. To Yvonne Farrell, DAOM, LAc, and Mikio Sankey, PhD, for holding up the lantern. To Charles, for coming to get me. To Ben and Maia Bridges, Gabriela and Cristian Chamorro, Isaac Chamorro-Hedrick, and Harper Smith, for inspiration. And to you, for courage.

Author's Note

My sister and I are only one year apart and, when we were young, people mistook us for twins. In some ways we still are very similar, but in others we're different. While I was jetting around the world pursuing travel writing and other spiritual quests, she settled down and had two fantastic kids. I tried to keep her up to date on what I was doing and learning, but so much of it was internal, and it has always been my way to process first and share as little as possible later. I wrote this book for her, as a way to bring her along with me.

While she may have a personal connection to my story, I believe it also has archetypal relevance. Everyone can (and perhaps will) experience something similar to what I've experienced (albeit translated into the specifics of their own lives), especially if they learn to listen deeply and trust their heart's wisdom. Don't let the seemingly extraordinary particulars of my story fool you: Otherworldly encounters, travels to exotic locations, and smooth finances are not key components to spiritual awakening. Inclination is a much greater necessity, but even that may not be crucial as we approach the so-called one-hundredth-monkey tipping point: the time when, simply by sufficient saturation, our culture will shift into a global (or even intergalactic) perspective, one that understands and embraces our interconnectedness.

I speak about this shift as if it were inevitable because I believe it is. In Chinese medicine, it is understood that yin or yang at its utmost reverts into its opposite. Another way of saying this is that things are darkest before the dawn. As the planet moves more deeply into crisis, so does its salvation grow ever closer. Many people believe that this turning point will occur in 2012—and it tickles me that this book will be published in that year. I've always been fascinated with the Maya, though I haven't followed the scholarship and interpretation that surround their wonderful calendar. Whether or not something grand and obvious happens according to that schedule, I think there can be no doubt that it is time to love and respect ourselves and our planet in ways that support us all.

Unfortunately, awakening to a more connected consciousness isn't easy, mainly because the process doesn't usually start until things get bad enough to require the shift. In my case, being at odds with my husband about whether or not to have kids was the terrible, wonderful vise powerful enough to crack my ego. But it could be anything that causes your world to fall apart—having a sick kid, unemployment, a hurricane or flood, or anything that requires courage, trust, and, ideally, a sense of humor. It is my belief that meditation, the Inner Child exercise (described on page 82), or another tried-and-true spiritual technique will help immeasurably when you find yourself at such a crossroads—but stories help, too.

Because I underwent an awakening process largely outside any one particular spiritual tradition, books and stories were crucial in helping me piece together what was happening to me. It is my hope that this tale may help others bypass some of the doubts and confusion that inevitably arise when we transition from one story of the world to another. It is for this reason that I share this book with not only my biological sister but all my sisters and brothers out there.

—Stella Osorojos
September 2011

Contents

Prologue

Camellia* was well-mannered, intelligent, and the daughter of a schoolteacher—someone, in short, with whom my mother liked me to play. This fact would have been fatal to my friendship but for another quality that Cam possessed in abundance, a wild creativity. She was always conjuring the most incredible scenarios and adventures for me and another neighborhood girl, Evie, to act out, which we did with relish.

The stage upon which Camellia, Evie, and I enacted Camellia's games was our whole neighborhood, a range that included the woods behind Camellia's house; every backyard we knew to be unwatched in the housing development where Evie and I lived; the entire pond behind my house, which we accessed, entirely unaccompanied by adults, by paddleboat or canoe; and all the nearby woods and fields, including a research parcel held by the University of Rhode Island, as well as an old boys' camp called Saint Dominic Savio. Saint Dom's star attractions were a derelict indoor basketball court ankle-deep in bird shit and an outdoor altar built into a constructed hillside where a creepy and angelic statue of Mary ministered to the robins and grasses. What more could three preteen girls ask for in life?

The kind of shenanigans that Cam liked to dream up were mostly innocent. She would take us out excavating for Indian artifacts in the buried trash pile behind her house and insist that the bits of old worn glass that we found were treasure-worthy. For a time, she would make us watch disgusting slasher movies but, because she was so high-strung, she couldn't watch them directly. Instead, she would stare at the TV's reflection in my eyes, compounding the creepiness factor by a millionfold. When we hiked out to that old Mary statue in the field, she would tell us to lie on the altar and pray for a miracle. We hoped to see tears spring out of her marble cheeks or,

---

*For the sake of privacy, some of the names in this book have been changed.

even better, for stigmata to appear on her outstretched hands, but they never did.

One winter, after the pond behind my house froze over, Camellia led a charge to the island in the center, inhabited, she told us, by a mean hermit. We never found out if this was true, because Evie fell through the ice before we got there. I was lagging behind, so I didn't see this, but she and Camellia returned with the tale. Cam had saved Evie, Cam recounted, with a stick that providence had placed within close reach of her heroic hand. As she spoke, her words billowed out with the ring of truth and both girls' cheeks were flushed, but they didn't seem so wet as all that. Believe me, it was entirely within the realm of Cam-possibility that she made up the whole story for my benefit. There is no doubt that Evie would have willingly played along, as I would have.

One summer afternoon, Camellia announced that she had a new plan for us. We would form a group, kind of like a gang, but nicer. Our group would have a name: "The Star Sisters." Then, with a tremor in her hand that made me think (before I dismissed the possibility as ridiculous) that she was nervous, she pulled something out of her pocket. In her palm were silver stars, the kind that her mother put on her students' exams. Cam told us that we were to put these on our forehead, in the space between our eyebrows. Again I heard a little quaver in her voice, and I realized that, yes, she was in fact nervous.

I immediately perceived a golden opportunity. Camellia was queen of the hill. My mother might have argued differently, but I knew that she was smarter and prettier than I was. She was also one year older, which gave her a distinct advantage in the coolness department. And here was a crack in her armor. With one cutting phrase, I could take her down. I could say that what she was suggesting was for babies. I could say she was queer, the word we used back then to checkmate each other.

But the truth was, I was thrilled by her plan. I loved the idea that she would include me in her group. I loved the sound of our name, "The Star Sisters." Every cell in my body responded to her request with a resounding *Yes!* Judging by the sparkle in her lively green eyes, Evie no doubt felt the same way.

With her hand still wobbling, Camellia handed us the stickers to put on our forehead. I stuck mine on immediately and felt a strange opening. My forehead seemed to expand around the star, a kind of yawning, *wah-wah-wah* feeling that I'd never felt before. I remember being almost lifted out of my body. It was a bright summer day, but I could feel the presence of the blind stars above us. It was as if I were touching them through this connection in my forehead. I didn't have the slightest idea what any of this could possibly mean ... or portend.

CHAPTER 1

Intuition and Acupuncture

Every summer weekend, Providence folk descended upon Narragansett Beach, the southern Rhode Island beach I grew up on. They rocked a look we called "guido," characterized by gelled-up bangs, layers of blue eyeliner, and lots of gold jewelry. Their bodies were hard, tanned to within an inch of leather, and they lay on towels, chewed brightly colored gum, and fussed with their leopard-print or shiny metallic bikinis, but never went in the surf. To me, they seemed like otherworldly beings, curious, fascinating, carrying the answers to unimaginable questions.

At the other end of that beloved beach was a cove carved out by the tides of an inlet known as Narrow River. There, then-healthy beds of seaweed supported a different but equally marvelous population of creatures. Eels darted between strands of kelp, and clustered on the shore were horseshoe crabs, prehistoric visitors who did their best to ignore us. To get to that idyllic spot, you had to wade against the Narrow River current, sinking into the soft wet sand and feeling the wavelets curl away from your ankles and shins.

Beyond its obvious pleasures, the beach was a place where I could read or be with my own thoughts. At home, I was a reader and a daydreamer, forever trying to find a quiet corner in which to do one or the other. Being internally focused from a young age taught me to identify what intuition was.

It happened on a day I was supposed to meet my neighbor to ride bikes together. Before heading out, I had developed a strange, unidentifiable feeling that I shouldn't go, but reasoning that this premonition didn't make any sense, I went anyway. The results were disastrous. When my friend's brother found out that she had been planning to use his bike, he reacted by punching her in the face with a closed fist. I was horrified to witness what amounted to a beating. Once safely back home and with time to reflect, I realized how valuable the information I'd received earlier had been. I vowed to pay attention when that knowing came again.

When I was about sixteen and packing for a solo trip to Colombia to visit my father's family, intuition returned. About nine o'clock at night, I got the heebie-jeebies and knew that something awful would happen if I got on that flight the next day. I explained my concerns to my family, and it was finally decided that I would go the next day, but that my stay would be cut shorter than planned. When I got home from the trip, we learned that a bomb had gone off in a building that one of my uncles, knowing that I was interested in architecture, would have taken me to visit if I'd stayed.

A slightly different type of intuition came some years later, when I was living with the man whom I would soon marry. Aaron had been away on business in London and he was late getting home to New York (where we were then living). I started to get more and more anxious, especially as the evening turned into night with no sign of him. Finally I went to the window, hoping to see him drive up in a cab. As soon as I looked outside, I heard a voice in my head that was distinct from my normal thoughts. For one thing, it was a different pitch than my own voice. For another, it seemed to shoot into my head from the outside rather than originating internally. The voice said, "It's not Aaron."

I knew immediately that Aaron was safe, though I couldn't shake the feeling that something was wrong. Aaron got home about an hour later. The flight had been late and, as nobody had cell phones back then, there was no easy way to call upon landing. I went to bed not knowing what the voice's message had been about, but early the following morning, Aaron's mother called with the terrible news that his brother Jeff had died. He'd had a heart attack at just about the time that I was freaking out and wondering where Aaron was.

My dreams were nearly as rich as my intuition. At college I went through a period where I was "waking up" in my dream and able to look back at my body. I could even walk around the school and discover things that I would then be able to corroboràte in my waking life. I later learned that this was similar to "lucid dreaming," which is practiced in order to empower the dreamer. At the time, it just scared the bejeezus out of me and I forced myself to stop doing it.

The point is that, by the time I became an adult, my relationship with my intuition was strong and I paid attention to what my dreams told me. This is the only way I can explain why I listened when a combination of dream and intuition told me to leave the best job I could imagine having.

Growing up, I had journeyed alone to visit family in Colombia and Switzerland, and every time I returned, I was somehow changed. Whether I'd seen slums, tasted guinea pig, or gone topless on a beach, my boundaries had shifted. My personal mutability fascinated me, and self-exploration became a calling. I loved travel. There seemed to be something inherently valuable in asking, "Who am I here? And here? And here?" So when I landed a gig as an editorial assistant at *Condé Nast Traveler* magazine, my first job out of college, I was ecstatic.

While the subject captivated me, I also loved working in magazines, especially under the tutelage of editor-in-chief Tom Wallace, who would later become the Editorial Director of all the Condé Nast titles. A natural teacher with an inborn generosity, Tom made a point of schooling his assistants in the editorial arts. In between arranging his calendar and calling his cars, I learned from him how to pick cover lines, balance the features well, even understand *Traveler*'s business strategies.

Despite what most people presumed, the *Traveler* staff didn't usually travel all that often. The feature stories were generally reserved for name writers, and the rest of the assignments went to reporters on location or with an established beat. At the time, I didn't mind this so much because I was learning tons and happy to be moving up as an editor.

The other great advantage of being at *Traveler* was that it allowed me to meet Aaron, who was then the Special Projects Editor. I remember poking my head into his office for the first time and being hit by an intuitive one-liner that said, "Oh, he's my kind of people." That said, I was definitely not interested in Aaron romantically, and this was for the best, since we soon began working together on Condé Nast's first Internet venture, *Traveler Online*. The intuitions of others were perhaps working better than mine on this point, however, because rumors started flying that we were having an affair about a year before Aaron and I proved them honest.

Once *Traveler Online* launched, the political situation in the office changed. Aaron was given a package to leave and, instead of floating to another magazine, he joined an Internet start-up called Agency.com. Meanwhile, I resolved to quit *Traveler* and go backpacking around Europe. I didn't want to leave Aaron, but neither did I want an office job for the rest of my life. When an associate editor job in the "Honeymoons" department at *Brides* magazine opened up, a position that required lots of travel, it seemed as if someone had heard my need to cut loose and provided me with the perfect avenue.

Working at *Brides* was a cushy gig, one that had me flying nearly every other weekend and becoming a connoisseur of the world's luxury hotels. Besides visiting many of the Caribbean islands, I also got to cover Mexico, Chile, Argentina, and French Polynesia. In every location I could feel myself becoming a different creature, and I couldn't help imagining what might unspool if I stayed. I could blend in with the crowd in Buenos Aires. I could open a restaurant in Todos Santos. I could dress in pareos and teach scuba diving in

Tahiti. So often, it felt as though any of those choices were a whisper away from happening, making it all I could do to board the plane bound for home. I didn't always like feeling so untethered, but I did enjoy learning about all the possibilities out there. If life is our creation, then our available palette is decidedly unlimited.

I'm sure everybody is restless in their twenties, but travel writing accelerated my discontent. I was dining in expensive restaurants, sleeping in celebrity digs, testing all variety of plush terry robe, compiling a short list of piña colada favorites (the Hotel Bora Bora's arrived in a glass rimmed with toasted coconut)—and yet, something was missing. Every TV show, magazine article, and pop song tells us that the dollar buys happiness and contentment, but that wasn't what I was finding. The more I consumed, the emptier I felt. Furthermore, recommending five-star hotels to young couples that could barely afford a single night at Disney World left me feeling dirty, like I was lying for a living. I knew I had more to contribute than that.

Up until this point, my whole life had been privileged. My family was intact and relatively happy; I'd never wanted for anything; I had tasted the world's luxuries. But something inside me hungered for more—and, early on, experience had conspired to show me that I wouldn't find it in the prevailing mainstream American ideas about what brings happiness. After probing the source of my dissatisfaction, I realized that I was frustrated by not helping people in a more direct way. To the best of my abilities, I wanted to serve humanity.

Not that I knew how or what to do about this desire. There aren't many opportunities for travel writers, and I'd already enjoyed the best of them. If I wanted more, I'd have to come up with something completely new.

This was my situation when I had an unusual dream. One morning, in the middle of all this intense turmoil surrounding the question of what to do with myself, I shot up out of bed simply knowing that I had to be ... an *acupuncturist!* I didn't remember any other specifics about the dream, but the quality of my knowing what my next career path should be was distinct: I just knew.

I'd never received acupuncture or even known anyone who had. I'd once seen a *60 Minutes* episode on the topic, where Chinese neurologists performed open-brain surgery using only needles for anesthesia. Beyond that, I was in perfect ignorance about the subject. My father was a doctor, as was his father, and I had toyed with being premed in college, so there was a thread that made logical sense to me, but mostly this impulse came from left field. I trusted it precisely because I knew it was coming from that intuitive place.

While *I* may have trusted my gut instincts, not many others did. My mother, who had chirped "Delta Dental! Delta Dental!" when she learned about Condé Nast's benefits package, told me I was making a big mistake. So did more than a few of my former colleagues. In some cases, the concerns were for my career as a writer, but others simply considered acupuncture to be quackery and hated to see me associated with something so dubious. Since my only argument for doing this was that it felt right, I had no choice but to weather their disdain with alternating bouts of bemusement and chagrin.

Despite the flak I caught for giving up a perfectly blessed travel-writing career, I never thought about changing my mind or caving in to peer pressure on the subject. Instead, something about standing up for myself, for my true self—an important function of my intuition—felt seriously good. Though I no longer lived by the ocean, I still felt at home wading against the current.

Within three months, I had quit my job at *Brides* and begun an acupuncture degree program part-time. Imagining all the spare time I would have between classes, I also started writing a novel. This was something that I'd always wanted to do, and it made the leap into an entirely different field seem more palatable.

I knew I was being ambitious, but I didn't realize just how ambitious. In traditional Chinese medicine (often called TCM, as well as Oriental medicine, never mind the political incorrectness), there are twelve primary meridians, more than three hundred and sixty acupuncture points, some four hundred herbs (to start with), and all sorts of patterns and pathogenic factors to learn. That's not even counting the theories layered upon theories, all rooted in a worldview that couldn't be more different from my own. Oh yeah, and much of the terminology in Chinese.

In the beginning, studying Chinese medicine is all memorization. You cram what seems to be pure silliness into your brain and hope that some day it'll make sense. Patterns like "Dampness affecting the spleen," "Internal wind stirring," and "Phlegm misting the mind" are considered legitimate conditions. And you're meant to keep a straight face when discussing an organ called the *San Jiao,* or "Triple Burner," which is an imaginary organ but nevertheless considered a force in the body. (What?)

Despite all the seeming preposterousness, one day it clicks. You realize that the metaphors upon which Chinese medicine is based, constructed from resonances found in the natural world, are just ways to communicate what was being seen in the body over centuries of observation. This contrasts with Western medicine, which focuses on the gross pathology of advanced disease states, making its scope very narrow in comparison with the whole-body view of Oriental medicine. Traditional Chinese medicine teaches its practitioners to really look and listen to the patient—the whole patient—and, in this way, to perceive subtle deviations from health. This is what accounts for its renown in preventing disease.

I loved studying Chinese medicine, not to mention all the Western subjects we had to learn, including biology, chemistry, physics, anatomy, physiology, etc., but it left me no time to write. This shouldn't have been too much of a problem—the degree takes four years, and there was no rule saying that I couldn't pick the novel back up after finishing my studies—but writing was something that had become part of my identity. Continuing to study Chinese medicine at the expense of writing, even for a short while, threatened my conception of myself. It all added up to one big internal conflict.

In retrospect, I see that this period of my life was providing me with an opportunity to expand my self-definition, an opportunity that I didn't take. Previous to the intuitive prod to become an acupuncturist, I'd always envisioned myself being a writer. Following through on the Oriental medicine degree would lead who-knows-where. Of course, leaping into the unknown is a tried-and-true technique for spiritual development, but I didn't know that at the time. Instead, I just knew that staying in school was highly threatening to my ego. If I was, always had been, and still wanted to be a writer, then what the heck was I killing myself at acupuncture school for?

At the same time, Aaron was doing phenomenally well at Agency.com. They were gearing up to go public, with the promise of Internet millions coming our way. Though that fortune never actually materialized, we did live on its fumes for a few years, and Aaron loved being able to offer to support me while I finished my novel. I felt incredibly honored to be given such a gift. Putting aside feminist ideas about not relying on a man, not to mention my confusion about my life's path, I quit Chinese medical school and dove into my novel.

Perhaps it really doesn't matter which path you choose. If I had stayed in grad school, I might have finished my degree sooner. And if I had finished my degree in New York, then who is to say that I wouldn't have still needed to devote time to writing afterward?

One thing is certain: Any direction you take leads back to yourself. For me at that time, that meant *confusion*. Though a part of me had always dreamed of writing full time, I found that the reality of it totally sucked. Instead of being able to delve into my project with complete focus, I developed an insidious pattern of procrastination and self-loathing broken only occasionally by desperate and sloppy productivity. In the mornings the whole day stretched out before me. What did it matter if I first spent an hour reading the newspaper? Or two? What did it matter if I made myself a leisurely breakfast? Then I'd sit down at my computer and … surf the Internet for two hours. Then it would be lunchtime. You get the idea.

Of course, there were days that I did get work done, despite myself. And it was fun. Or it would make me cry, which was even more satisfying. I was writing about an awkward preteen girl who was actively trying to get her horse to throw her in order to overcome her fear of falling. When she finally did manage to get herself tossed, I had a cathartic realization that there really are doors of perception, à la Aldous Huxley and Jim Morrison. As the main character was flying through the air, she had a vision of her dead mother, and it occurred to me that she had found the doorway to the realm of spirits. I sobbed for days after making this discovery. And yet, I also had the distinct impression that there was something I was missing, something I didn't quite understand about what I had written. A voice was whispering, just beyond my hearing.

Though moments like these seemed to make up for the days of frustration, the sheer number of difficult days was overwhelming. I'd never realized how completely wild my thoughts were. I could set out in the morning with all the willpower in the world and still get sidetracked for hours by the most inane celebrity detail being presented as news on Internet sites. It led me to start questioning what this propensity of the mind toward dissolution is all about.

In particular, I wondered what it said about the creative process. Was I supposed to let my thoughts wander? Perhaps the ensuing chaos would seduce the artistic muse to my side. Or was I supposed to buckle down and force myself to put word to page? Cultivate extreme discipline and focus, with a stick if necessary? This second option seemed kind of harsh. Perhaps it was all the crying I was doing, but I had an instinct to be nicer to myself for a change. As an experiment, I decided to let my mind wander where it may. I hoped that, after a while, my mind might settle down naturally, but that never happened. Instead of wandering around until it reached some exhausted bottom, my mind just continued to spin and spin. I felt helpless and at its mercy, as if my mind itself were the wild horse I was supposed to be writing about and I a tamer with no tools.

This became a very black time. Aaron was working long hours, and I was home alone in a sun-starved apartment trying to manage my mind with a wet-noodle philosophy about discipline. Becoming multimillionaires—which we did, at least on paper—when Aaron's company went public didn't help. The world's distractions were simply that much more accessible. Something had to change, and since I didn't know much about meditation at the time, I looked outside for that shift.

When the opportunity came to leave New York for Los Angeles for Aaron's work, I jumped on it.

CHAPTER 2

California, a Shaky Time

Before packing up and flying to Los Angeles, Aaron and I decided to get married. Because we had been travel writers, it seemed fitting that we should get married in some far-off locale that we'd not previously visited. An astrologer that Aaron and I sometimes visited recommended Japan—and the prospect did have a certain appeal. For one thing, neither Aaron nor I had ever been there. Second, it was famed for its gardens, which seemed a proper sort of thing to tour on a honeymoon trip. But the clincher was that we had just painted a mural of a Japanese landscape on our living room wall, in the area that a feng shui expert had called our "relationship corner." Had the astrologer somehow sensed this? Had we somehow invited the suggestion by doing so?

Whatever the reason, Kyoto it was. The tour operator we contracted to arrange this trip had contacts at Daitoku-ji, a temple complex in the hills to the north of the city. That's how we ended up on our wedding day in a centuries-old Buddhist temple called Zuiho-in, learning to meditate for the first time ever.

I say that we "learned" to meditate, but since our monk was speaking in Japanese, it was really more like we gleaned an idea about it. From what I could make out from the monk's undecipherable sounds and sharp hand gestures, we were supposed to sit up straight, touch our tongue to the roof of our mouth, and not move.

Any further nuance was beyond me, but I didn't care. The wide hall was stunning, with *zafus* and *zabutons* set upon two long daises, each one backed by enormous windows that looked out onto spectacular gardens, where songbirds seemed intent on charming the September maples into turning red. It was the easiest thing in the world to sit there for an hour, soaking it all in.

After the meditation session and our beautiful wedding ceremony, the abbot served us tea and talked to us for forty minutes. I couldn't understand his Japanese either, except that, with him, I almost could. Somehow I knew what he had said even before our translator had done his job. He told us that he had never performed this type of ceremony for Westerners before, and he gave us two bits of advice that we especially remember: First, that when we fight, there is nobody else there, so really we are only fighting with ourselves. And second, that there was no telling what this experience would lead to for us.

While I sensed truth in these sentiments, I couldn't help feeling like there was something that I wasn't quite grasping. His words had an underwater quality, as if I were hearing them from far away, perhaps my own depths. Though I struggled to tease out what he could possibly mean, it would be some time before I started to understand what our wonderful abbot was really hinting at.

When we got home, I wanted to continue meditating but I didn't. At the time I berated myself for my laziness, but perhaps that's not the whole story. I've come to suspect that gestational periods are part of the process with spiritual growth. Sometimes just planting the idea of meditating (or whatever) is enough for a while. After a certain amount of time, the ambition will poke its head up naturally again. A start-and-stop period may follow until, finally, one's commitment sticks and the practice is established. I can't say why this seems to be common, only that it does.

Meditation is very difficult for Western minds, used to constant stimulation, to commit to. Be it TV, radio, Internet, advertising, whatever—from the moment we get up in the morning to the time we go to bed (and sometimes even later than that, since I know many people who can't fall asleep without the TV blaring at them), we absorb massive amounts of stimulation. This is like caffeine for the mind and leads to addiction. If it didn't, then the thought of spending an hour a day unplugged from it all would seem like a wonderful respite, but for most people an hour of quiet meditation is about as appealing as spending a week in the desert with no hope of *agua*.

At first, I was no different. Once Aaron and I got home, I learned a little bit more about meditation and tried again. This time the object was to count my breath. Invariably, it went like this: inhale, exhale, one; inhale, exhale, two; inhale, exhale, three … and then my mind would wander. It didn't matter if I was thinking about nuclear physics or peas, my thoughts would stray—and it could be fifteen minutes before I even remembered that I was supposed to be counting.

This loop-the-looping was actually frightening. I couldn't believe how wild my thoughts were. I knew that I had a hard time buckling down to write, but now that I was really looking at the problem, I could see that my mind was like some crazed ferret on crystal meth—and that I was utterly at its mercy. Unfortunately, this deeply unpleasant revelation did not convince me of the need for meditation. Quite the opposite: It pushed me away from the practice. Again, this is possibly a result of Western conditioning, whereby instead of cultivating persistence and valuing effort and the small gains we make along the way, we're encouraged to be superstars or nothing. We throw in the towel before we even get over the initial hump. Anyway, I certainly did.

Busy-ness is another great American virtue. Besides being "bad" at meditating, I was also, I told myself, too busy for it. For a while, perhaps I was. When we returned from Japan, there were parents to tell about our elopement, parties to plan and attend, and then we had to pack up our New York apartment for California.

Though thinking about leaving New York was stressful—it meant leaving behind friends and family, as well as the magazine and new media industries that had nurtured us—at least we knew that we could always return since we had no plans to sell our apartment. At the same time, we were excited about the housing possibilities in LA. By the end of my time in New York, I was feeling seriously pinched by living with almost zero access to the earth. We had been looking for a new apartment with a garden, but they're pretty scarce in New York and, as the Internet bubble began to implode, our supposed capacity to pay for such a luxury was dwindling rapidly. I knew this itch would be much easier to scratch in the sprawling City of Angels.

The first day we drove around trying to find a rental, Aaron took me up to Beachwood Canyon. He thought I would be charmed by the little village at the base of the development that originally advertised itself with giant letters set into the hillside spelling out its name: Hollywoodland. He was right, I was. We vowed to look for a home in that neighborhood.

Then, as intuition would have it, on our way out of the canyon, I asked him to turn down a street called Cheremoya. That's the name of a tropical white-fleshed fruit, one that I knew from my trips to Colombia, where it is made into popsicles that my Uncle Manuel loved. Though I myself never developed an appreciation for the flavor, it still sounded like home.

About halfway down on the left, a "For Sale" sign was posted out in front of the cutest little bungalow I'd ever seen, with a placard outside that identified it as the original Beachwood Canyon schoolhouse. I caught my breath and blurted out, "That's it! That's our house!" I jumped out of the car and was delighted to discover that the inside matched the exterior promise, with a lofty feel and windows that looked out onto a Japanese garden. It was perfect.

Unfortunately, when we checked with the real estate agent who was handling the property, she informed us that the owner had no desire to rent. If we wanted it, we would have to buy it. This would mean selling the place in New York—and *that* would mean having to take a leap of faith.

For one thing, we were by no means assured that if we did sell our place in New York we would be able to buy the Cheremoya house, since the owner was unwilling to strike a deal with a contingency. Losing our toehold in Manhattan for no particularly good reason seemed heartbreaking, not to mention financially idiotic. Second, neither of us had a job in LA, nor any particular hope of one. Even if we did get the Cheremoya place, we couldn't necessarily be assured of being able to pay for it on an ongoing basis.

It was a nerve-wracking time. I felt as if I'd been tossed up in the air and didn't know where or when I would land. But that's what leaps of faith feel like, and they seem to be an important part of opening up to a spiritual path—how else can you explore the unknown?

There's a Native American story about taking leaps of faith called "Jumping Mouse." In it, a mouse has heard tell about a great mountain. He aspires to reach it, though none of his kind has ever seen it and they all tell him that it's too dangerous, that he'll die if he tries to find it. He searches anyway and, eventually, he reaches a wide river. He knows that he might perish if he jumps in but, encouraged by a frog, he does so anyway, gaining the name "Jumping Mouse." Midleap, Jumping Mouse sees the great mountain but then splashes down into the water. Despite the big belly flop, he now knows that the mountain really does exist and he can chart a course for it. His spiritual quest has started, one that could only begin in earnest after taking that initial leap of faith.

I didn't know about Jumping Mouse then; I just felt confused and lost. In desperation, I found myself consulting the *I Ching*, the oracular eastern Book of Changes, for the first time. We had bought a copy of the famous Wilhelm/Baynes translation of the ancient Chinese "Classic of Change" after our New York astrologer advised Aaron to meditate with it. He hardly ever used it, but nevertheless it made the cut when we were packing for LA and, one day, shopping at the Pasadena flea market, we picked up three Chinese coins, one of the tools used to divine answers from the fortune-telling book.

Perhaps it was the newness of those coins that prompted me to turn to the *I Ching* that particular day. All I know is that after spending some time figuring out how to use the forecasting method, and feeling like I had nothing to lose, I asked the *I Ching* what would happen with the house. The answer it gave was unequivocal: It basically said, "There is a house in your future." I was stunned that the book could answer my question so pointedly. Here was a twenty-five-hundred-year-old text from the Zhou Dynasty telling me about my personal life!

Sure enough, just as the *I Ching* predicted, the seemingly impossible came to pass. The sale of our stock remnants came through, another buyer dropped out at the last minute, and when we called the owner of the Cheremoya house to put an offer on it, she accepted our bid against two others. Besides being thrilled that we were getting our little house in Beachwood Canyon, I found that the incident rooted the *I Ching* in my heart and gave me confidence in its power.

Eventually I would come to trust that book as much as my own intuition, but before that could happen, I needed a reason to turn to it. That happened when my life began falling apart.

One quiet morning in September 2001 just after we'd moved into our new house, a friend of mine called up. Knowing that we had no TV, she said we better turn on our Internet: The Twin Towers had just been hit by a plane. My old college roommate happened to be visiting from New York (she lived in lower Manhattan), and I'll never forget the sight of her standing in her pink underwear, crying amid boxes in my otherwise empty living room. As we watched, a second plane hit the towers, and they collapsed.

For months after the tragedy, most of the world was continually bombarded by the 9/11 images and tales. Of the planes crashing. Of the debris. Of the workers sifting for bodies. Of the smell. Without a TV, we were spared much of that and I'm glad of it. Rehashing trauma only serves to reinforce it in our minds. We're capable of remembering and honoring the dead without having to damage ourselves in the process.

Even without excessive exposure to the national grieving process, Aaron and I both absorbed stress from the tragedy, as I'm sure we all did. But those catastrophic events weren't the only cause of stress in my life. When I left New York, I had let much of my freelance work languish in favor of finishing my book. After the third draft of the thing, with still no elegant resolution in sight, I wanted to take a break and so I dove into writing screenplays. Aaron and I wrote one together. And then I wrote another. And then another. While we had some success with them (we placed in a couple of contests, and then I got selected for a special yearlong screenwriting program at UCLA), agents and movie deals weren't exactly camping out on our doorstep. Not generating my own income was getting to me. And I wasn't getting any younger.

The "not getting any younger" part was especially difficult around the question of whether or not I wanted to have children. I'd always said I didn't. During kindergarten, I sat in the sandbox and told my best friend Sara so. But around age thirty-two, my feelings changed and I was suddenly seized with the desire to see a toddler padding around the house. Trouble was, I had married a man who had no such inclinations and who really couldn't fathom my change of heart. To him, having children meant the end of our ability to travel freely, the end of our disposable income, the last stop on the coolness train. I suspected that the vehemence with which he protested against the idea indicated some deep-seated trauma, but he didn't agree. This made me angry with Aaron, but I also mistrusted my own feelings about wanting to have a child. It felt as though my uterus were urging me on, not my mind. I wondered if, in the long run, I wouldn't be happier resisting my biology.

To think of this now, I am amazed at how undercutting of myself I was. It never occurred to me that my uterus might be voicing the desires of my heart or vice versa. (They're similar structures, after all—both hollow, muscular, and capable of nourishing a child.) Or that either one of those organs could and should be trusted over the guidance of the brain, which sits far away from the more centralized processing centers in the enteric nervous system and cardiac muscle.

Of course, the mind/body split I evinced then is by far the norm in our society, where it's next to crazy to suggest that we should value the information from our heart and gut—known in Chinese medicine and Daoism as the *Shen* and *Dan Tien,* respectively—over that of our brain. When I discussed my dilemma with friends, not one asked me what decision might *feel* right, or what my gut instinct said about the matter. We all discussed the pros and cons of having kids, going 'round and 'round, never able to cut through the morass the mind is capable of creating—because that's the great beauty of the brain: It can see all sides and talk us into or out of anything. Conversely, the *Shen* and *Dan Tien* create the knowing that arises *before* thought. They're what engender intuition and guide your true path—provided, of course, that the volume in your brain is turned down enough to be able to perceive their messages!

Concurrent with this spike in my desire to have a child came the precursors of thyroid disease, though I didn't yet realize it. I only knew that I was gaining weight, my hair was changing texture, and I was growing depressed. Driving back from yoga class one day with Aaron, I saw this clearly. He was talking about something perfectly innocent, but it was annoying me. As I struggled to control the snipey comment that jumped automatically to my lips, I realized that I was doing it all the time—that my thoughts had become an incessant downer that I was constantly battling.

With no career, no kids, and increasing depression, I knew I had to do something. When I found out that *Architectural Digest* had an assistant editor position open, I applied, though the job was a peg or two lower than what I'd left in New York. They offered me the spot, but when I asked for a salary that was at least commensurate with what I'd left at *Brides,* they subsequently rescinded the offer.

Humiliated and crushed, I felt boxed into a corner. The only way out seemed to be turning back to the acupuncture degree I'd left behind in New York. It wasn't that I loathed the idea; I had loved the subject, but I didn't seem to have any other choice since I couldn't make anything else happen. Sometimes life has to drag you kicking and screaming toward what's best for you. It's not necessarily the most fun way to go about finding your destiny, but it is effective!

At least, I reasoned, the dream that had started my acupuncture quest would finally be answered. Because I'd had such a clear knowing about what I was supposed to do, ignoring that premonition now seemed wrong; it went against all my early efforts to listen to that inner voice. I felt as though there might be something behind my getting that degree that I had yet to discover. And life had conspired to ensure that there was no other choice than to finally find out what it was.

CHAPTER 3

What Health Looks Like

As soon as I decided to swim with the current instead of fighting it, the synchronicities began to appear. As it turns out, California was the perfect place to finish an acupuncture degree since it has the most stringent licensing requirements of all the states. A degree from there can be transferred easily to nearly any other state in the country. Another detail that seemed auspicious was that the logo of the most convenient acupuncture school near me, Emperor's College, was made up of the Chinese symbols for the numbers 3 and 8, which had been my favorite since childhood. For as long as I can remember, I've played with numbers in my mind, noticing when the lucky ones show up and where; adding and subtracting them until they appease me; generally obsessing. Suffice it to say that a 3 and an 8 being the symbols of my chosen grad school felt like more than coincidence.

Before picking my studies back up again, I made two deals with the universe. If I finished the degree, I wanted to be assured that I would somehow get back to writing. I envisioned myself writing about acupuncture and alternative medicine for magazines. Second, I insisted that my experience in acupuncture school be filled with friends. The first time around I had not been privy to the bonds that form through long study sessions because I was attending part time and quickly fell out of my cohorts' schedules. Without that kind of help and support, I knew I wouldn't get through.

I say that I "made these deals" with the universe, but that isn't really the case. The New Age concept of "asking the universe" for what you want, à la the cult-hit movie *The Secret,* wasn't really a part of my consciousness at the time. I was making a deal with "them," but I couldn't have told you who I thought "they" were. In fact, I wasn't even fully conscious that this was my thinking pattern. I only realized it later, after my continued unraveling finally drove me to see a psychotherapist. In one early session, I casually told her about these grad-school stipulations that I had made and she asked me with whom had I made them? I had to confess that I didn't really know. Looking back, I see this as another example of a split that was going on inside me, one that would ultimately have to be healed.

Within the first month of school, a health crisis hit. After class one day, my eye started hurting. It felt as if hot needles were poking the medial edge known as the inner canthus—not just an ache, more like cover your eye and shout, "Ow!" Worse, my vision became blurry on that side, though this symptom came and went. I made an appointment with my primary-care physician.

In the days before my appointment, I remembered that an astrologer back in New York had warned me that something was going wrong with my eyes. She had given me the name of a doctor whom she thought I should see, but my insurance didn't cover that particular MD, so I went to my own and he hadn't found anything. As I'd had no symptoms at the time, I forgot about it. Now I wondered if I shouldn't have taken her specific recommendation more seriously.

While the excellent ophthalmologist that my primary-care physician recommended couldn't find anything wrong with the eyeball, she agreed that my right eye was protruding slightly, a condition called exophthalmia that's frequently associated with a form of thyroid malfunction known as Grave's disease. She suggested that I get my levels checked.

When I went back to see him, my primary-care doctor discovered that although my T3, T4, and TSH levels were in line with what the Western world considers normal, I was producing antibodies to my thyroid hormones. This finding suggested that it would be only a matter of time before I would need thyroid medication, which I would probably be on for the rest of my life, though my MD could do nothing for me until my levels became abnormal. I would have to wait for it all to get worse before he could prescribe any sort of treatment.

When I went home and looked it all up on the Internet, I was horrified to discover that, within the Western paradigm, the exophthalmia would be allowed to get worse and worse until surgery could be justified. Then they would operate, pull out the eyeball, remove one of the bones in the back of the socket in order to make more room for the protrusion, and pop the eye back into place. Even if I hadn't been in Chinese medical school, I'm sure I would have resolved to find some other solution.

During this time, I woke up one night in the middle of a bizarre dream. Or perhaps I was still dreaming: The hot drone of LA summer was in my ears, and my room had a yellowish cast that unsettled me. Where was it coming from? As I looked around, I realized that I was floating near the ceiling.

As soon as I understood this, I started drifting down toward my bed, vaguely aware of being watched. Hieroglyphic images flashed through my mind and, simultaneously and seemingly on autopilot, my right arm began tapping points on my body in what I inexplicably knew was some sort of locking or unlocking code. Particularly because I was studying Oriental medicine, this intrigued me. What points would have this sort of function? Why was I touching them? Then I realized where I was and what I was doing—and a numb horror shot through me.

As if responding to the alarm, my "body" dropped precipitously down to my bed. My consciousness slipped back into my physical body and, as I began to open my eyes, I realized that one was already ajar. My right eye was staring out toward the bedroom door—and seemed to have been doing so all night.

Above me, I could feel a vague presence, perhaps above the roof, perhaps still in that dream. To get away from it, I jumped out of bed and raced for the mirror above the sink. My eye was dry and pro-truding; I was becoming a close cousin to Frankenstein's hunchback butler, Igor. What the heck was happening to me?

Back in my bedroom, I suppressed the urge to look up at the presence I felt hovering there, sure that I would have to confront something that I really didn't want to see. Trying to calm myself down, I reached for the book that had comforted me before: the *I Ching*. I hadn't thrown the coins in a while, but now I did, asking very simply, *What is going on?*

The response said something like "Friends are here to help you. Stay calm and don't ask them to go away." I had just woken up in the air performing what seemed to be some weird ritual on myself, my eye was bulging out of my head, and I was entirely freaked out by the prospect of anybody being in the room with me, let alone "friends" who might be the cause of all this strangeness. Although the *I Ching* was admonishing me not to ask "them" to go, I thought I'd never heard such a good idea! Shaking my fists in the air, I asked whomever was there to leave.

The drone that had been filling my ears diminished at once. In a hid-den corner of my heart, I knew exactly what had just happened. I had been taken up to some sort of extraterrestrial "ship" and was somehow being helped. With a subdued sadness, I realized that I had probably just missed a phenomenal opportunity. But a larger part of myself felt that ETs, ghosts, etc., were *scary*, not to mention seriously un-chic. I simply couldn't become one of those weirdos who went around crazy-talking about their bizarro encounters with what seemed more like the limits of their own sanity than anything truly otherworldly.

Rather than scrutinize this experience, I simply ignored it. It existed in my mind as a silent storyline, an underground river with powerful currents that I was aware were working on me, though I never talked about them. I had plenty else to occupy myself and let it do so gladly.

As students, we were encouraged to receive acupuncture regularly in order to enhance our learning experience. With thyroid disease looming, my motives for getting treatment were doubled and I went weekly to my school clinic. While I loved getting the needles, which didn't hurt and even produced a nice buzzy feeling that usually induced a restful nap, I didn't necessarily like what my practitioners were telling me. They said that if I wanted to be truly healthy, I might want to get off the birth control pill and quit drinking so much red wine. (It's true; I loved the vino nearly as much as I loved cooking, which was a lot. And they go so well together!) They also suggested that I start taking Chinese herbs.

Have you ever seen Chinese herbs—the kind you boil down to a black ink that fills the house with a bitter stink that lingers for days? Despite their horrible taste and the messy chore it is to brew them, they can be quite beautiful: A relatively commonplace pre-scription might include a handful of smooth bupleurum twigs, some bright-red goji berries, a tongue-depressor-shaped stick of yellow astragalus, shaved licorice roots with their sweet smell, pieces of sour peony root or bark, and a smattering of dried chrysanthemum flowers and mint leaves. Before processing my own prescriptions, I always take a moment to admire the earthy beauty of nature's apothecary. This helps fortify me for later, when I actually have to swallow the stuff.

While the herbs I started taking were hardly delicious, there was something about them that I began to crave. At my school, they said this was a mark of my needing them, the idea being that the body's own ability to heal itself is intrinsic, though perhaps dormant. By listening and paying attention to what feels nourishing, one can identify one's best medicine.

For a while this was all I had to go on. I was getting acupunc-ture weekly and taking my concoctions three times a day, but there seemed to be no dramatic change in my symptoms. It wasn't until I'd been on this regimen for six months or so that I finally realized that, little by little, I was actually getting better. My depression was gone; my weight had normalized; my eye pain had lessened. After another year of less diligent herb-taking and acupuncture-going, I found that my eye pain receded to the point of being a light pressure. There are certainly no bone-removal surgeries scheduled for my future!

I have come to consider this slowness of action to be one of the greatest strengths of Chinese medicine. By diligently replacing needed nutrients at the cellular level; by gently steering the great ship that is the human body with these tiny oars that look like needles; by applying firm, subtle pressure week after week after week after week, the body can grow into health in the most natural of ways, with the firmest footing at its base. It's the same principle behind bonsai, where gentle shaping over time results in the greatest beauty.

Unfortunately, nothing could be further from the expectations that most Westerners have regarding health care, where they demand pills that promise to knock out yesterday whatever is bothering them today—even if it's a chronic disease they have and not a flu bug; even when they've done years of damage to their body by smoking, drinking, overeating, and leading highly sedentary lives; even when they know, because their regular MD has already told them so, that the main answer to their problems is that they quit doing all those things. Still, they presume that acupuncture doesn't work if it doesn't change everything in the first three sessions. This isn't to say that acupuncture can't have immediate and powerful effects, only that its slower mode of healing should be understood, too.

Does all this sound like I went ahead and did the unthinkable? That I gave up drinking red wine? I did. *Sigh.*

I also added *qi gong* to my healthy regimen. I was already doing yoga, but after taking a *qi gong* class at school, I was hooked. A martial art considered to be the precursor to tai chi, *qi gong* teaches slow, gentle movements that augment the body's energetic and bio-magnetic fields. I love feeling the energy flow through my body the way it does after practicing. I could always tell when I'd had a good session back then because my painful eye would start tearing, presumably moving out some of the stagnation that continued to be there. It certainly felt that way.

Another guy in my class, a dear friend, had a similar reaction. By the end of the first week of practice, he began crying all the time. Not weepy tears, just water flowing down his face. He is a tough Jew with big muscles and a blustery attitude, so it was highly annoying to him to be breaking down all the time, but that's one of the things that can happen when you start stirring up the body's energy.

Qi gong doesn't always start the water works, though. My classmates had all sorts of different reactions to moving their energy. One girl had to go to the bathroom all the time. Another developed a pulsation in her *Dan Tien,* the area below her belly button. She showed it to us in class—it was actually visible beneath the skin!

As I continued with *qi gong* practice, I eventually learned a form called the "Primordial Meditation." The way it was taught to me, one imagines a column of warmth penetrating down to the heart as one exhales, and eventually down into the *Dan Tien.* We were supposed to practice this for twenty minutes, two or three times a day. Almost as soon as I began, I felt grief pouring out of my body, endless amounts of grief, as if I were a clown pulling emotional handkerchiefs out of my mouth. When I asked my teacher what was going on, she told me to carry on, that it was working.

One morning while I was practicing in bed, I felt all the energy that I'd been drawing down to my lower belly whip around and surge back up my spine to connect again with the front side of my body. It was the most extraordinary sensation. I felt light and energized, positively buzzing. Friends whom I encountered later in the day said that I looked like I was glowing from within.

Later I learned that this was an experience of inner alchemy, the kind of thing that famously concerned the Daoists (East Asian philosophers who understood the connection between man and cosmos) and that can be found in all the great religions. It's the kind of thing that's traditionally not talked about because, by having expectations about what is supposed to occur, the likelihood that it will occur is diminished. This is a *watched-pot-never-boils* phenomenon and it's a real concern. At the same time, I think it's important to have an idea of why it can be so healing to practice these alchemical arts and to be able to draw encouragement when nothing seems to be happening with your own *qi gong*, meditation, or prayers. It will—as long as you focus on the practice and not on the benefits.

And, yes, I finally started meditating. Some of my teachers at grad school were suggesting that meditation was at least as important as traditional Chinese medicine itself—maybe even more so. I was impressed by their passion. The New Year's Eve after I started graduate school again, Aaron asked me what I would like from him for the coming year. I told him that I'd like him to meditate with me in the mornings, and he actually agreed. We started getting out of bed twenty minutes earlier than usual, sitting on cushions that faced our garden, and counting our breath. Having him alongside me made it so much easier to get going.

Even though my thoughts were still a wicked cross between ferrets and hamsters, I actually saw results from meditating within the first month of regular practice. Aaron agreed. By the third week our memories had noticeably improved; we could recall things with much greater ease. We were also more even-tempered with each other. Even my natural shyness abated. I'd always been somewhat tongue-tied, but soon after I started meditating, my speech patterns smoothed out, losing the rototilled quality they'd previously had. We were astonished by how much of a difference this simple practice was making.

Inspired by our meditation, I went to see the Dalai Lama when he spoke at UCLA. He was charming and funny. Everybody listened with love and, when the talk was over, began filing out with decorum. As I waited in the bleachers for the throngs to clear out, my eyes fell on the retinue that had accompanied His Holiness into the auditorium. Amongst the dozen or so red-robed monks, one was in utter bliss, with his face upturned and light filling the space around him. I was struck by his appearance and looked closer. Why did he seem to be so much taller than the other monks? Why were they crowding around him? It almost looked as if they were trying to shield him.

I tried to find Aaron to point the fellow out to him, but he was too far ahead in the crowd. When I looked back, I saw what the monks were trying to hide: The one in the middle was floating above the ground, his robes swishing under his feet. Though people were mingling all around, nobody else saw this. I stared, goggle-eyed, but the monk's feet never made contact with the linoleum as he was shuffled out of the hall like a living, helium-filled balloon.

Maybe I was mistaken and the hundreds of others who apparently saw nothing were not, but what if he was floating? Was it possible that nobody else could see him gliding along there because it was simply so unexpected? What else do we miss by being unwilling to see? And to look? It was one of the first inklings I had that more might be possible than I'd imagined.

This period was a great time of learning and expansion for me. I'd always rolled my eyes when I heard New Agers wearing flowy skirts talking about how "It's all about energy." Now I sat there in acupuncture class thinking, "Oooohhh! It's all energy!" It didn't make me go out and buy anything sheer or purple, but it did stop me from feeling quite so threatened in the presence of anyone with bells in her hair.

I was also deeply engaged by the mysteries I sensed unfolding around me. The secrets of these rich inner traditions were mine to explore—and I did so with eagerness and relish. In retrospect, I've always had this esoteric hunger, something that articulated itself in a dream I had when I was on the verge of adulthood, maybe sixteen years old.

In the dream I kept asking a single question: What is the answer? In pursuit of the answer I came to a river where the bridge was out. I knew I needed to get across, but there were stinging nettles in the water so I couldn't swim. A Rasta man waded by and I climbed on his shoulders. Once he had deposited me on the other side, I still didn't have the answer, but I did have a lesson that I'd learned on the way. I put this in the pouch at my side and then undertook another mini-adventure. In every scenario I gleaned another lesson, which I put in my pouch, though I still didn't know what the answer was. Finally I had this bag that was full of lessons, but I was still frustrated by not knowing what the answer was. When a woman in black robes appeared, I knew that she knew the answer and I implored her to tell me. She would only smile. No matter how I pleaded, she simply smiled. When I woke up, I realized that although I still didn't know what the answer was, I did have all these life lessons that I'd gathered along the way—and that they were all I need to know to learn what the answer might be. Quite miraculously, I did in fact seem to be on the trail of the answer.

Inevitably, the process of letting in more light leads to some of it shining on the dark places. For me and Aaron, that meant the sensual arena. Suddenly our sex life was a mess. For one thing, that pesky desire I had for a kid was not abating. Nor had Aaron's interest in such an endeavor sparked up. We had previously enjoyed a fun and lighthearted connection through lovemaking. Now we circled each other warily and made love awkwardly or not at all. For one thing, I often felt betrayed when Aaron approached me for sex. I felt like he wanted the part of sex that pleased him, but not the piece that would fulfill me. Aaron, I'm sure, just wanted things to go back to the way they were before.

Making matters more complicated, I had quit taking the birth control pill. It is thought by many alternative medicine types that the disruption it inflicts upon the body's natural cycles causes problems in the long run—problems (like thyroid difficulty) that implicate an off-balance endocrine system. If birth control pills really could be a complicating factor, they were an easy one to reverse.

Of course, it would be disingenuous of me to suggest that I did not have ulterior motives in going off the pill. What could better force the kid issue with Aaron than putting the onus for birth control on him? It was a weak jab, indicative of how helpless I felt to make any more devastating decisions.

Not that Aaron was unaware of my real motivation. He knew very well what I was up to and called me on it. We talked about where we each stood and we tried to understand each other, at least as much as was possible when my feelings were so mishmash and his were so hidden. Our ability to talk honestly with each other was what kept me in the relationship. Even if I disagreed with him, I had such a good friend in Aaron that it was hard to imagine life without him.

Why did Aaron have such an aversion to fathering a child? Every time I brought up the subject, which was now a lot, a black pall came over his face. He acknowledged that it might have something to do with his relationship with his father, which had been close but complicated. His father had been a pathological liar, left the family when Aaron was fourteen years old, and died six years after that. He had also made no attempts to hide his preference for Aaron over his other son, Jeff, which caused Aaron some guilt. Beyond that, there were concerns about overpopulation and the environment, the difficulty of life on this planet, the financial pressures. Mostly, though, Aaron could only say that he just didn't want to.

When the idea of Aaron getting a vasectomy arose, I felt split—in more than two pieces. On the one hand, I thought it was possible that, once temptation was taken away, I would be able to put the idea out of my mind and go on with the life we'd originally envisioned together. Don't forget how much conviction I'd had for so many years about not wanting kids, not to mention my distrust of my body's own instincts. I could imagine a scenario in which Aaron getting a vasectomy repaired our ability to connect again through lovemaking, allowing us to start rebuilding from there. On the other hand, I knew it might push me away from him irreparably. It seemed just as likely that he would get the vasectomy and I then I would leave him.

I shared these concerns with Aaron and he told me that whether or not he was with me, he knew he didn't want to have children, and that he would go ahead with the vasectomy. In this cold light, I saw that I had no choice but to support him as a person on his own path, whether or not it included me.

CHAPTER 4

The Anger Button and How to Press "Delete"

Immediately after the vasectomy, I took care of Aaron as he walked gingerly around the house. Things seemed relatively calm. But after a while, I noticed that I was no longer holding in check a tendency that I had to be snappish and short. I was getting angry and annoyed at Aaron for the smallest things and felt totally at a loss to contain any of it. Aaron mostly responded to my bitterness by walking out of the room, infuriating me even more.

I seethed and felt desperate ... and seethed some more.

I considered leaving him, but many things kept me rooted. There was the fact that I was still in school, what my parents would say, etc. Mainly, though, I didn't particularly want to leave Aaron. I didn't want to destroy all that we had together, I just wanted to augment it: I wanted a child with him.

Our meditation practice was becoming increasingly important, and it was something we shared. A few years after the wedding in Japan, we had started reading about Buddhism—texts like Sakyong Mipham's *Turning the Mind into an Ally*, Stephen Batchelor's *Buddhism without Beliefs*, and Sogyal Rinpoche's *Tibetan Book of Living and Dying*. Also, we developed a relationship with a Zen center in Santa Fe, New Mexico. After an anniversary trip to 10,000 Waves, a Japanese spa surrounded by piñon and juniper, we had gone to meditate at a temple run by the awesomely dynamic Roshi Joan Halifax. It is called Upaya and, pretty soon, we became members.

These tools convinced me to try looking inward instead of raging outward and, over time, I came to realize that I'd had problems with my temper since much earlier in my life. Looking back, I could see that I'd been angry since adolescence and puberty.

You see, my mother and father didn't handle my coming of age very well—at all. As the second of four kids, all born within five years, I hadn't bonded much with either of my parents, who were generally either busy with my siblings or away at work. As I said, I grew up reading a lot and making a world of my imagination and was often left to that. I was seen as the "easy" one.

By the time I approached my teenage years, I was used to being somewhat ignored, except on the most obvious level, such as through my grades or what other parents and teachers said about me. Then I started experimenting with drinking and drugs. And boys. And my weight became a preoccupation. I'd been chubby as a child and didn't want to be any longer. I started to exercise and that led, through the advice of a friend, to bingeing and purging behavior. When my parents cottoned onto this, they reacted with hysteria, pushing me away even further.

Part of what was so frustrating about my parents' over-the-top reactions was that they could only see the most surface level of what was going on with me. Through an arts camp that I attended in the summer, I was discovering that I wanted to be a writer. The teachers there all thought I had promise, and I started writing poetry as a form of self-exploration. My dreams were often vivid, sometimes even grotesque, but by turning them into poems I could learn something about myself. I became dedicated to this process as a lifestyle.

My parents knew I was starting to write, but they had no way of knowing how important it was to me. Or that my adventures with illegal substances grew out of an interest in learning about the nature of my mind. More often than not, I approached these substances from an almost anthropological perspective, trying to figure out why Kerouac and Kesey and all those hippies from the sixties had thought they were so important. For the most part, I was concluding that such drugs weren't for me.

My nascent relationships with boys were complicated by the fact that my father is old-school Colombian. If he'd had his druthers, he would have locked me in my room until I was ready for marriage. At the same time, he bought my older brother a Mercedes and encouraged him to bed as many blondes as would have him.

When I accused him of a double standard, my father agreed, saying that that was the way things were going to be in his house. I was a reflection of him, he said, and his reputation was more important than who I might be becoming. When I turned to my mother for support, she wouldn't go against my father. To say that this devastated me would be an understatement. If I had felt unseen before, now I was a ghost, a furious one.

As happens in the therapeutic process, some obstacle—in this case, Aaron's unwillingness to have a child with me—triggers earlier feelings. If Aaron hadn't lit the fuse, then I'm sure something would have eventually come along to help me identify what a strong hold these old hurts retained on me. But his particular "betrayal" cut right to the heart of the matter for me, making me feel unloved for who I was, which, in one regard, was a woman. Though it wasn't fun to come face to face with those repressed and unresolved feelings, it was better than ignoring them and letting them continue to work their corrosive alchemy on my body and soul.

Perhaps part of the reason that difficult emotions were emerging in our life together was because we finally knew how to address them—as opposed to the old cut and run. Our meditation practice and Zen readings were pointing a new way through conflict, one that resonated for both of us. Ideas about calm abiding were at the forefront of our consciousness. As we sat each morning, we tried to watch whatever thoughts or feelings arose and release them. We weren't necessarily successful with it—that's not the point—but we didn't stop practicing.

Over time, this seeped into our lives off the cushion. If we started to argue about something, eventually one of us, usually Aaron, would detach and walk away until we could converse again with greater calmness. In the beginning, as I said, this infuriated me. I thought that, at best, he was being holier than thou and, at worst, completely obnoxious. Over time, though, it changed the way we fought, training us to maintain perspective even as we discussed deeply difficult problems.

Besides figuring out how to work with our reactions and not become possessed by them, we were learning about the nature of interpersonal relationships and even of reality itself. Aaron was intrigued by Carolyn Myss's book *Sacred Contracts,* which offers an expanded perspective about why we encounter and get involved with the people we do that he hadn't previously considered. And my acupuncture studies were seriously augmenting my thinking about the world.

Traditional Chinese medicine builds upon an understanding of the relationships between macrocosms, like the seasons and the elements, and microcosms, such as the body, applying the lessons and examples of one to the other for illumination. From fifth grade I'd trained to be a poet, so metaphor was an easy pool to dive into. The hard part was overcoming the Western viewpoint that denies any pervasive unity in the world. But once the evidence became overwhelming, I did indeed start to see how my life might be a reflection of the greater world, and vice versa. A perception of myself as an interconnected being began to emerge.

In terms of my relationship with Aaron, my developing sense of interconnectedness extended to him. I wondered if our Japanese abbot, who had said that when we fight there's really nobody else there, was right. It occurred to me that I might just be fighting with myself. That made the thought of leaving Aaron seem futile. If I wasn't getting what I wanted within my chief relationship, where I had a partner willing to mirror my bullshit back to me, it didn't seem likely that I would get it alone—and not just because what I wanted was a child.

It all came to a head one day while I was sitting in our study. I was writing something and my mind wandered. I started thinking again about what an asshole Aaron was for not helping me have a child and all the ways that his refusal injured me. I started getting madder and madder and thinking about what I would say to him if he were there. The fact that I knew what he would do if I said anything—which was to remain calm—pissed me off even more. I could actually feel the anger boiling in me.

And then … I noticed myself noticing this.

The amount of anger that was coursing through my body was appalling.

My heart was racing. My fists were clenching. My eyes were searching wildly around the room. I was out of my mind!

This couldn't be healthy, either for me or for him. Even if I were justified in being angry with Aaron, the amount of bad feeling I was processing had to be toxic.

I took a deep breath.

Then another one.

It occurred to me that I could make a choice as to whether or not I wanted to continue having this amount of anger.

I didn't.

Aaron didn't really deserve it. He didn't deserve to live with what I was generating—nobody does!

I realized that, if I wanted to stay, I would have to find a way to forgive him.

And if I couldn't, then I should leave and spare him my abuse.

That moment in the library chair was huge for me. My meditation practice had given me just enough distance on my emotions to be able to distinguish them as something not intrinsic to my "personality," but as something I was capable of mastering. I finally had the mental space to be able to see my anger—and could therefore decide how to act on it.

This amounted to my beginning to have control over what some energetic anatomists call "the emotional body." There are different descriptions of what it looks like, but Barbara Brennan gives a comprehensive view in her book *Hands of Light*. The emotional body is what we use to process and express emotions—and it is seriously deranged in many people.

Pop culture provides many examples of just what a berserk emotional body looks like. Mel Gibson's tirades, Lindsay Lohan's breakdowns, and Charlie Sheen's implosions are examples of the emotional body running amok. On some level, these people are lovable and likely hurting, but presumably functioning at the mercy of their emotions. Sometimes emotional incontinence looks more like the ego. Sarah Palin seems to have some deep-seated need to be noticed that can often look calculating, but I'll bet that there's an emotional wound underlying any strategizing she does.

It's a great shame that we aren't taught to better control our emotional bodies during our adolescence. Eckhart Tolle, who writes about one aspect of the emotional body as the "pain body," provides some great suggestions for how to do this. For example, he asks parents to identify the pain body as a separate entity by naming it. This helps children to understand that they are not their emotions, which is the first step toward exerting control over them. I think it would be equally beneficial to teach children any technique such as meditation that helps them create space around their thoughts.

The ability to recognize and work with my own emotional body didn't come instantaneously. After that moment in the study, I had to keep practicing. It was a process of catching myself in the middle of an emotion (which is hard at first!), taking a deep breath, and making a choice from a calm place about whether it benefitted me and others to continue expressing that emotion. Besides making life more pacific, this process eliminated a lot of the regrets I might have generated by saying things I would later have wished I hadn't and helped me curtail my habit of pressing "Send" on rash emails. Hallelujah for the "Delete" button!

It also helped me to see the true cause of my emotions. After letting my initial burst of anger dissipate, I started making it a practice to ask myself where the root of my emotion lay. More often than not, I realized that my anger was masking fear—very often fear for the person I was angry at. I began to see how my parents' often-hysterical reactions, which I had clearly inherited in my own form, were based in fear. Besides being better able to modify my own reactions, I also began to sympathize with my dear mom and dad.

Gaining control over my emotional body allowed me to start feeling tender toward Aaron again. In fact, I began to feel quite blessed to be in a relationship that nurtured my spiritual growth, if not my desires for a family. I still didn't know how things were going to turn out with my desire for a child, but at least I saw the value of being at loggerheads with Aaron about the issue. It seemed to be functioning as a crucible of spiritual growth for each of us.

This was just before my thirty-fifth birthday and, as was his habit, Aaron asked me what I'd like for a present. I didn't really need anything, but the question got me thinking about what I really wanted in my life. For some reason, the only thing that came to me was that I wanted to change my name.

I can't tell you how strange this was. Sure, I'd thought about changing my name when I was a teenager—doesn't everybody? But why would I think of that now? I put the idea out of my head.

As my birthday grew closer, however, and I continued to ask myself what I might like to do to celebrate it, the only thing that kept coming up was that desire to change my name. Even more confusing was the fact that this strange idea had a subterranean quality that was similar to my dream about acupuncture school. It smacked suspiciously of intuition and, by then, I well knew that if it was intuition, I would not be able to ignore it for long.

The idea that I might have to go ahead and change my name panicked me. What would my friends think? What would my parents say? I could imagine the look on Aaron's face if I told him—and I didn't want to see it.

Finally, Aaron repeated his question about what I wanted for my birthday. I screwed up my courage and confessed the awful truth. And there it was, that look of dismay; it flickered across his face before he could hide it away.

Then he took a deep breath and said, "Okay. Well ... what do you want to change it to?"

CHAPTER 5

Changing My Name

Confessing my desire to change my name and being met with equanimity, as Aaron did for me, was a blessing that amounted to being loved for who I was, crazy ideas and all. The idea of changing my name certainly did seem nutty to me. I just couldn't shake its association with people who are hiding something, or who are posing in some way, trying to manage their image to the outside world. Perhaps ironically, it didn't square with *my* image of myself.

Up until this point I had been a perfectly normal person named Laura Stephanie Chamorro. I'd always been sensitive, artistic, and interested in fringe ideas, but I'd never let a crack show in the relatively stylish, affluent façade I projected, an instinctive self-protection mechanism that I learned first being my father's daughter and then later, sliding through the halls of Condé Nast, where showing up to work in sandals with unpainted toenails was considered a serious fashion offense. Now I was contemplating total exposure, and it made me squirm.

As I was trying to screw up the courage to do something I couldn't explain but somehow knew I had to do, I finally hit upon the idea of changing my last name to Aaron's. I hadn't taken his surname when we got married. Now that I was feeling sweet on him again, the idea seemed appealing, with the potential to take care of this pesky desire

I had in a way that would likely pass external scrutiny relatively unnoticed. I liked the idea.

Here's where my numbers obsession comes in again.

As a writer, I often used a Kabbalah website with a database of baby names to develop characters. (The only thing I knew at this time about Kabbalah, the mystical branch of Judaism, was that Madonna was a follower.) I found its descriptions of what effects a particular name would have on a person's life to be uncanny. Persuaded by the site's accuracy, I thought it would be fun to check with the people behind that database to see what they thought about my name. From the site, I'd gleaned that different spellings of names were an important piece of the puzzle. I imagined that, at the outside edge of possibility, they might advise me to change the spelling of Aaron's surname—Sugarman—to Sugerman, or Sugarmann.

To my horror, the Kabbalah people had bad news for me. Their system simply didn't work like that. My given name was all wrong for me, as were all variations of "Sugarman." If I wanted to improve my life, I would have to change my *whole* name. The suggestions they gave me included such winners as "Merna Xenja," "Chellisa Morinski," and "Brawnnely Brawne."

Believe me, that would have been the end of that, except that their explanation for why I had to change my whole name was a numerological one. Their system was based on ideas about root numbers. In itself, that didn't sway me one way or another, but they were saying that, based on my birthday, my root number was 3 and that I should therefore have a "3" name. That hooked me, since, as I said previously, I'd been obsessed with the number 3 my whole life. More than ever, I felt the mysterious pull of this little project of mine. I knew I had to do it, even though the idea mortified me more and more the deeper I looked into it.

While I was agonizing, trying to figure out what to do, I hit upon a new idea. I was an artist, right? What if I changed my name as an *art project*? What if I blogged about the whole process? Then, at the end of the year, I could change my name back! I might even have enough material for a book! At least this strategy might be cooler than being *earnest* about it all. It was something that my friends and family might be able to understand. Was I rationalizing? Absolutely. I was so terrified then of expressing what was in my heart.

Once again, I turned to the *I Ching*. Its message left me shaking.

In a nutshell, it said that if I undertook this name change, all my wishes would be fulfilled. Whoa! *All of them?* I pictured a book deal, a baby, a pile of money to replace our lost nest egg. When I look back on what I envisioned, I can't help but smile. What I got in the end was so much more valuable than anything I could have then imagined.

My new first name came to me while I was sitting in the library. I had been looking through all my baby name books (ostensibly another writer's tool) but, not finding anything resonant, had put them aside. As I was staring out into the distance, willing something to arise, I suddenly saw letters that spelled out "Stella" hanging in the air. They were kind of gray and hazy, but definitely distinguishable. Realizing how strange this was, I blinked and the vision disappeared. I tried to reconstitute what I had seen, but I couldn't. Later, when I ran the name by the Kabbalah people, they got very excited.

"That's the perfect name for you! How did you find it?" they asked. I didn't know what to say and kept mum, but the synchronicity of pulling a name out of—literally—thin air and having it be numerologically correct made me feel as if I were on the right path.

My last name, "Osorojos," had an equally intriguing debut. After figuring out what components went into a good moniker for a "3" person, I had come up with a surname that was a combination of my favorite color (red), Aaron's nickname (Bear), and Spanish (actually, "Osorojos" is incorrect Spanish, but it worked numerologically). Still, I wasn't sold.

Then one afternoon Aaron and I were standing in our living room talking. He was waving his arms around, gesticulating broadly. Suddenly the dim lights seemed to flicker and one of his arms began to glow and pulse. I widened my eyes, trying to clear what I presumed was a problem with my vision, but the experience persisted. I got closer to see what was going on with his arm and, there, at the cuff of his new sweatshirt, was a logo that read "Red Bears."

I blinked again and this time I saw that I'd been mistaken: The logo actually said "Red Ear." But it was too late—I'd already gotten the intuitive message that "Osorojos" would be a good name for me.

Recounting this experience now brings up questions for me—and undoubtedly for you—that I didn't have at the time. Why did I accept these signs so readily? I was used to listening to my intuition, but this was a whole different level. Why didn't I flip out?

One answer is that the ephemeral quality of these experiences simply prevented me from holding on too tightly to them. As soon as they appeared, they were gone. I couldn't point out what I had seen to Aaron; I could only tell him about it. Then I had no choice but to let it go.

Also, the one thing I *could* take away from these experiences was the sense they gave me that I was on the right track. I simply didn't think that names would be suddenly appearing in the air in front of me if they weren't somehow divine. Aaron, who had begun studying Carl Jung, thought that these incidents of synchronicity suggested a larger framework; he believed they pointed to a collective unconscious. But that wasn't my thinking at the time.

Instead, I took it as evidence that there were beings out there who were helping me, though I didn't know who they might be. I was still decidedly not thinking about the extraterrestrial/acupuncture/eyeball dream. And though I wasn't averse to the idea of spirits or angels or guides, I didn't exactly have a working sense of them. My belief that I was being helped from some other dimension stemmed from a largely buried part of my consciousness that reached all the way back to my childhood.

When we're kids, it's not uncommon to believe in beings beyond the ones generally accepted by grown-ups. For me, it started with the presence of Mary. Raised Catholic, I just loved Jesus's mother, with her pretty face, her long brown hair, and her fluttering blue robe. Every time I got dressed for church, I knew she was smiling her love and light down upon me.

Mary's wasn't the only presence I felt around me. Sometimes when I entered a room, I'd feel as if somebody were there whom I couldn't see. Though I tried to dismiss these feelings, they were often strong enough to cause me to run out of the room.

Later in life, these occurrences seemed different. After Aaron's brother died, while we were at a memorial for him held at the radio station where he'd worked, I went into the recording room and was so nearly knocked over by what I perceived to be Jeff's spirit that I blurted out, "There you are!" I got the distinct impression that he was intensely embarrassed by all the fuss being made over him. I told Aaron what I'd experienced and he nodded and said that that sounded about right.

People may roll their eyes when the topic of ghosts or spirits comes up, but it's not that wacky. A quick Google search will tell you that one third to one half of Americans believe in such supernatural phenomena. The fact that these beliefs don't square with mainstream "scientific reality" doesn't seem to bother anyone. And it didn't bother me, either, though I was invested in the scientific worldview as much as any member of our postmodern culture, believing hook, line, and sinker any sentence that started with the phrase, "According to a new study...."

It was as if the two lobes of my brain did not communicate with each other at all. Once in a while, the logical/realistic side would wonder at the perceptions of the creative/mystical side, but not very often. And the creative side was perfectly happy to exist under the logical side's radar, functioning, picking up signals, and even acting on them, but never making its discoveries or beliefs fully conscious, content to exist in the shadows.

Once I had chosen a name and Aaron was on board with my plans, the next task was to tell my parents about it. I told them first because I knew that if they really objected, I probably wouldn't have the courage to go through with it. I presented the idea as I thought of it then, as a derivative of my desire to change my name to my husband's. The only catch was that I was changing it to something new instead of taking "Sugarman." I told them that Aaron might change his last name to "Osorojos" too, because at the time he thought he might, at least once he left his job.

To my great surprise, my parents received the news with good cheer, though my mother, in particular, sounded a little thrown. However, both she and my father recovered quickly, going on to say that they thought it would be cute of us to change our name. My father even teased us, calling us "Los Ositos," the "Little Bears."

When I hung up the phone, I felt as if I'd gotten their blessing. I was amazed to the point of wondering if they'd understood me, though I'd been as straightforward and clear as I knew how to be. I felt light and happy—like this whole name-change thing wouldn't be as hard as I thought!

Next on the call list were my brothers and sister and my closest friends from college. There, I got mixed reactions. My sister Pamela was definitely not in favor of my changing my name.

"You can call yourself anything you want, but I'm always gonna call you Laura," she said. She then added a "Sorry" that she immediately confessed she didn't mean. She's just like that—caring, brash, true to herself.

"That's fine," I told her, laughing, secretly relieved that not everything would be changing so quickly.

My brothers took my news more or less in stride. Jaime, my younger brother, giggled nervously and asked me what my parents had said, and older-brother Luis started developing a whole new line of corny jokes on the spot.

"Hey, if you combine your names, you'd be called 'Stellaura.'"

And, "Hey, do you know that there's already a kids' book *Stella Luna*? Since your dog is named 'Luna,' I guess this confirms that you're batty."

My closest girlfriend encouraged me to go for it—and for this, I was grateful—but almost every other friend was opposed. Sometimes they didn't tell me this directly, but it was obvious from the strained way they began dealing with me. Others were perfectly upfront about their disapproval. One friend told me she thought "Stella Osorojos" sounded like a maid's name. Another started jumping up and down, telling me not to do it. Another scolded me for putting such a burden on my friends, who knew me one way and for whom it would be hard to make the switch.

I must say that I was amazed at all the fuss. It made me realize how powerful names are—and how much we dislike change. But mostly I was shocked that anybody was paying attention. This whole name-change effort was something that emerged from my shadow mind, and I presumed (or maybe just hoped) that it would somehow retain that quality and pass unnoticed by outsiders, as everything else associated with that part of my life had always done.

A few weeks before my thirty-fifth birthday, which was the day I was planning to go to City Hall to file the paperwork for a name change, I called my mother to chat. When she asked what my birthday plans were and I told her, she started groaning.

"You're not really going to do that, are you?"

"Uh, yes."

"Oh, Laura."

"Mom? I told you guys about this weeks ago."

"I thought that was a joke!"

"Um, no."

"Wait, so what are you going to change your name to?!"

Gulp. "Stella Osorojos."

"Stella! You can't change your name to 'Stella'!"

"What? Why not?"

"You cannot change your name to Stella!"

"Mom, I've already decided. You guys said it was okay. Remember? Los Ositos?"

"You cannot change your name to Stella!"

"Why?"

"Because."

"Mom, you have to tell me why not."

"Because, Laura. Your father's girlfriend before me was called 'Stella.'"

"What?!"

"Stella de la Rosa. And she was not a nice lady! She was … an artist!"

My poor mother! As if it weren't bad enough that her first daughter, whose name she had undoubtedly chosen with great care, was betraying her in this way, there was also the teasing that this awful coincidence spurred my gleefully mischievous (and entirely faithful) father to commence.

While my heart went out to her, by then I'd already had my parents' support through the hard part. I'd taken their apparent approval and shielded myself with it as I told my friends about my plans. And I'd believed they were okay with it when I went even more public with the news, telling my patients and colleagues at my school's clinic. In some ways, that level of disclosure had been the most uncomfortable for me, since my acquaintances didn't know me very well, and I could only imagine the awful things they must have thought about me.

I apologized for causing my mother any distress, but I told her that I was going to go through with it.

On my thirty-fifth birthday, I woke up early. It was spring and the sun was shining. It seemed like a lovely day to change my name, but I thought it prudent to double-check with the *I Ching* before setting off. I had been using it more regularly since it told me that all my dreams would be fulfilled by changing my name, but I sometimes found its answers to be inscrutable. Not that day. After asking if I should go through with changing my name that day, I threw the coins and received a hexagram that counseled me to wait. It said unequivocally that, before taking any action, I should meditate.

Hmm. Okay. I'd built up so much drama around this day that this advice was a bit of a letdown. However, a bigger part of me was quietly relieved. The social fallout from my announcement had shaken my resolve, and I was happy to have time to absorb it all. I changed my plans for the morning and meditated for an extra-long time that day. I had the next morning free too, so I figured I would just go downtown then.

When the next morning came, however, I checked again with the *I Ching*—and it gave me the exact same hexagram. How amazing! I thought. With sixty-four different hexagrams and multiple ways of receiving each one, the odds of receiving the same hexagram for two days in a row are decidedly against.

Then, the astonishing happened: I received the same hexagram the next day, too. And the next. The day after that I received a different hexagram but with essentially the same message. In fact, for the next three months, I received only three different hexagrams, all with the same basic message—that I wasn't ready yet to change my name, that I should meditate more on the matter, that I should wait. The chances, I am told, of four times in a row are less than one in 250,000 and of receiving only three hexagrams in ninety days miniscule, less likely than winning Lotto three times in a row.

What the heck was going on here?

CHAPTER 6

Write What You're Scared to Write

The sheer preposterousness of the *I Ching*'s repeat messages thoroughly pleased me. The mounting odds against receiving one of only three hexagrams day after day convinced me that, without a doubt, something beyond what I could see was at work, though I didn't know what that might be. Like a kid in the back seat of a car, I was being taken along for a ride and there was nothing to do but shift into trust mode.

Being willing to trust seems to be another one of those tried-and-true steps on most spiritual journeys. The story of Jumping Mouse illustrates this repeatedly. When Mouse gets to the river and is told that to reach the Sacred Mountain he must jump, he doesn't ask why—he just does it, an act of trust that reveals to him his sacred journey. Once he gets to the opposite bank of the river, he meets a blind buffalo and offers him his eyesight without worrying about how he himself will get along without eyes. This act of trust allows the buffalo to shepherd Jumping Mouse across the plain, protecting him along the way from predators. He finally makes it to the great mountain and climbs it. At the top, Jumping Mouse is once again told to jump, and he does so without question. In his freefall, he becomes an eagle. This beautiful transformation is made possible because, in his faith and innocence, the world rises up to meet his inner trust.

A Zen story that illustrates this point concerns a Mr. Shang, an entirely naive sort. He lives in a town in which some bullies decide to do him in. They tell Mr. Shang a lie, that there is a pearl of great value in the bottom of a pool of water with deadly currents. Trusting them, Mr. Shang jumps in and, some moments later, reemerges having been untouched by the danger and carrying a giant pearl in his palm. Trust builds the world around us in its image.

In the reprieve that my waiting created, I focused on a blog that Aaron had set up for me in order to chronicle my name change. The name I had chosen for it, "Under the Pine," honored the giant pine tree that lived in our backyard. I was posting items as often as I felt moved to do so, writing about my mother's reaction to the name "Stella," conveying what my friends said, cataloguing my own feelings about it all.

As the days went by with no indication from the *I Ching* that I would ever be advised to change my name, I started to feel quite lost. What was happening? What was I doing? I'd initiated this whole transformation only to be stuck cooling my heels, waiting for a cryptic old book to release me. One day, feeling down in the dumps about it all—I still didn't have a career or a kid and now I had no idea whether or not my big name-change stunt would fly—I started contemplating what I really wanted from this process. I wasn't thinking about the surface reasons I'd planned to do it, but the deep-down and super-embarrassing reasons. Here's what I wrote:

> The fever (or astrological pull?) of wanting to change my name has passed. My head feels clearer. The cacophony of questions, "Why am I doing this? What do I hope to accomplish? Have I lost my mind? Do I really want to go through all this trouble?" has settled down and, in the clearing, I just step forward. I am doing this. I'll find out why later.
>
> I had all these results I imagined would come from changing my name, some seeded by the Kabbalarians. In the "Name Report" they compiled for "Laura Stephanie Chamorro," it was their contention

that my given names were at least partly responsible for the "sudden and extreme losses, both personal and financial," and "severe nervous tension" that I have, indeed, experienced. A name with a magic mixture of consonants and vowels would be "more balanced," they assured.

"Stella Osorojos" would never have a panic attack, I foresaw. "Stella Osorojos" would not flub an Internet fortune. Furthermore, "Stella Osorojos" would move to Santa Fe. She would open an art gallery. Can't you see the lowercase font on a storefront window? "osorojos"—there's art inside!

Or, I know! "Stella Osorojos" the book! I'll change my name and I'll start a blog and everybody will read it! And then! Then all the years I've spent squirrelled away, writing and writing, will mean something! A project! An intriguing project! A life!

As I finished, I suddenly started shaking. What I wrote doesn't seem so bad to me now—just honest. But at the time, I found it to be mortifying, like confessing that I was nothing but a phony and a fake. My pretentiousness was nauseating. This project wasn't some cool art thing, it was me trying to erase the fact that I felt like a loser!

And what if I pushed the "Publish" button by mistake, posted this to my blog, and people actually saw it? I had told everyone—all my college friends, all my former Condé Nast colleagues, all my family—about my blog and many of them were reading it. Tom Wallace could be reading it! Editors who might still be inclined to throw me a bone were reading it! If I published this, they would all know how pathetic I was.

Worse, I could never call myself "Stella Osorojos" if everybody knew how puffed up that name was. My whole plan would just flop—and it would be a big public flop. What would I have if I didn't have "Stella Osorojos"? I didn't feel like I could go back to calling myself "Laura Chamorro." I would be nameless. In some very tangible way I would die.

Trust is necessary on a spiritual path at least partly because one has to get through that period of turmoil known as "the dark night of the soul." A term familiar to most spiritual traditions but mostly linked with Christianity, it has to do with the necessity of the false self dying so that a purer version of oneself can be born. It is an experience at once both epic and intensely personal. From the outside, the form the crisis takes may not look like much, or make any sense. But for the person in the midst of it, it's like staring into the abyss of your worst doubts and fears, feeling utterly abandoned by your god or gods. In my case, the whole period leading up to this moment could be seen as my "dark night of the soul," but this moment in particular, facing this existential annihilation, was crucial, though I didn't know this at the time.

Instead, like a ghost brushing past my ear, I simply heard the words "Write what you're scared to write." They came in the voice of my very first writing teacher, Dave Anstaett, for that was one of his most treasured dictums: "Write what you're scared to write."

Well, that seemed like a bad idea.

A very bad idea.

And yet, it spoke so truthfully to my heart that I couldn't brush it aside.

"Write what you're scared to write."

So I pushed the "Publish" button.

It's very hard to describe what came next. I was still sitting in the same chair I'd previously been in, but I had the distinct sense that I was floating. It was silent and I was very much at peace. I suddenly knew with utter clarity that I was neither Laura nor Stella, nor any identity that I had ever or would ever construct for myself. At the same time, I knew I was still me. It was as if I'd been crow-barred out of myself into something simpler or purer, certainly bigger.

This was a different sensation than the feeling of having objective distance on my emotions, such as when I'd learned to control my anger toward Aaron. Here, added to the ability I'd gained to be watchful toward my emotions, was an ability to view my ego with a degree of detachment, something I'd never done before. If a sentence was going through my mind, it was this one, over and over: "Oh, I am not my name!"

The immediate effect of this was something like shock. I stayed in my chair for as long as I could, nervous that this feeling would go away. It seemed to me that nothing and everything had changed. I was not my name, not my story, not my lineage, not my past, not my future. I was not Laura. I was not Stella. I was not dark-haired. I was not smart. I was not a loser. I was not an artist. I was not my father's daughter. I was not a student, nor a writer, nor a wife, nor childless. I had never been any of those things, though I'd never seen that before. I was something else completely, and all of those adjectives were merely part of the story of "Laura" or "Stella" or any other name I would ever choose to give myself.

I did know one thing, though. In that instant I knew with unshakeable clarity that I am a spiritual being. I had awoken to this fact.

Then things got really weird.

As I sat in the study in total wonderment, I pondered who else knew that we are larger than our stories about ourselves. Did everybody know except me? Or was it more likely that most people didn't know? I had no idea. It seemed like it could just as easily be either.

With questions crowding my brain and needing to move, I got up out of my chair. As I made my way to the living room, I was oddly nervous that I would not be able to hold on to these realizations, even to the point of feeling like I shouldn't tilt my head too much. I felt that tenuous.

At the time, my living room was a wide-open space with a dining table at one end and, on the other, a couch sitting atop a giant Chinese art deco rug. As I stepped out past the couch, there in the middle of the carpet, in almost the exact center of the room, I saw a locust. I'd never seen such an insect outside the house, so its presence inside, when all the windows and doors were shut, was doubly startling. As I stared at it, trying to figure out what it was doing there, I suddenly saw something odder still: The locust seemed to have multiple bodies, all stacked on top of each other, going up and down like the layers of a cake.

When I blinked my eyes and tried to clear my vision, the locust lost its hard layered effect, but for some reason I could still perceive its apparent multidimensionality, like the echoes in a raindrop or the many images in a fun-house mirror. There was the locust, with its tan shell and folded wings, just as it always looked. But all around were its reverberations in other levels of existence.

In each dimension outside its physical embodiment, the locust was shimmery to the point of seeming like no more than a refraction of the light. I almost wished this were the case, because in one of the farther-out dimensions the being took on a more menacing cast. Its intelligence seemed fierce and it emitted a flat malevolence.

I knew at once that it was a negative extraterrestrial. And that it was unhappy with the self-discovery I had just made.

And, yes, this is where I totally lose it.

I realized that the insect in my living room was actually a creature wishing me harm, and then I was flooded with other startling revelations. I knew that it had been the one keeping me in the loop-the-loop of my egoic identity. It had accomplished this through some sort of control over my brainstem. And it had effectively been enslaving me in order to feed off my energy.

Whoa.

As you can imagine, this was way too much information to process all at once. Part of me wanted to run and hide under the covers in the bedroom, while another part thought I was being entirely ridiculous thinking that a one-and-a-half-inch bug was such a threat—a bug!

Now, if you were peering in the French doors to my living room at that moment, I expect that you would have seen an ordinary midthirties woman ogling an equally ordinary insect, not some epic encounter with a beastie from outer space. So I can't blame you if, right now, you're thinking that what I'm describing was a hallucination of some kind. Perhaps it was. But my experience was that I was seeing the truth for the first time, as if the rest had always been the illusory part.

Odder still, I was able to perceive these two versions of what was happening, though doing so strained my mind's ability to make sense of any of it. I could toggle back and forth between the old "reality" and this new one that I had so recently discovered. I could decide to see the locust as simply an insect or, if I chose, I could include an expanded understanding of it, like seeing the cells that make up an organ, or the organs that make up the body.

This gave me the ability, to some extent, to decide which version of "reality" to trust, and I had just made up my mind to shoo the silly bug outside when it seemed to pick up on my intention and leapt toward the front door. Once I'd ushered it safely outside and told it never to come back, the darn thing just turned around and glared at me. It looked, for all the world, as if it knew how to bide its time.

CHAPTER 7

The Truth about My Heart

Alone again in my living room, I paced up and down. I wanted to call Aaron, but the only messages I might deliver sounded insane:

"Hi honey, I'm not my name!"
"Hi honey, we're all being sucked on by extraterrestrials!"
"Hi honey, my brain exploded today!"

It was all way beyond the bounds of reason. Though a part of me had always been more or less comfortable with ideas about ghosts and guides and what-have-you, to be confronted with the thought that extraterrestrials might actually be real, or at least more real than I'd previously imagined, was earth-shattering. To come face to face with what seemed to me to be a real live one was beyond threatening—it crossed the line. And I didn't like it one bit. It shook every pillar and foundation in my mind and life.

I'm pretty sure that most people can sympathize. Though one CNN poll reported that 64 percent of respondents believed that aliens have contacted humans, most people—91 percent—told the pollsters that they had never actually had contact with aliens or known anyone who had. In other words, the concept of ETs? No problem. A meet-and-greet with one? Mind-blowing!

My brain felt as if it were tearing into pieces and it was all I could do to maintain any semblance of composure. I really didn't want to become one of those people who talk about extraterrestrials. On the other hand, the pressure of my discovery was immense. It had torn the fabric of my reality and was threatening to rend it completely. The fear of losing my marbles was almost as great as the terror I felt contemplating the extraterrestrials themselves.

Worse, my revelations kept compounding. As I waited for Aaron to get home, my dark ideas grew longer shadows. I realized that the whole history of the world that I'd been told was a complete fiction, that everything in the textbooks I had read in high school was, at best, only part of the story. I realized that negative extraterrestrials had come and subjugated us. They had done so by raping women, instilling ideas about class and social structure, then enslaving us with thought-control devices that kept us locked in addictive patterns of anxiety and fear.

Later I learned that much of what I was perceiving was almost exactly what former BBC newscaster David Icke had been reporting in books and videos since the early 1990s, to great ridicule. I myself was deeply skeptical, even as the realizations poured in. As these ideas arose, my mind was simultaneously grabbing at every possible reason to reject them. For one thing, where did ETs come from? The whole world couldn't be fooled, could it? How could I *know* these things when nobody else I knew seemed to know them?

Then something at least as miraculous as everything else that had happened that day occurred. I was on the verge of going completely gaga when, casting around for anything firm, anything stable and believable to ground into, I stumbled upon the truth about my heart. I realized that although everything around me might be in utter chaos, I could always trust my heart. Unlike my brain, which was subject to the influences of TV and faulty textbooks and perseverating tendencies, the guidance of my heart would never fall under the aegis of anyone or anything but myself. As long as I listened— truly listened—to the whisper of my heart, I would always be fine.

I don't know where this idea arose from or what gave me the confidence to trust it. It just seemed like the truth—and not only that, but the *only* truth, as if the world were made up of beings, each with their own heart axis, each with a guiding light of their own. For a second I questioned this idea, too. It seemed that, given how malleable the world had just become in my mind, this notion might be as shaky as all the rest. But something—fear? prudence?—told me to grab on to this lifeline, at least for the time being.

Calmed sufficiently to give it a try, I took a deep breath and centered myself in my heart. The world stopped spinning enough for me to relax, just a little bit. Each breath was another moment of calm. When I veered off toward panic again, I brought my mind back to my heart and breathed into it. Once again, meditation had given me crucial space and perspective.

Moments passed. The sun was still shining outside. The walls of my house seemed to remain tangibly solid. Then, to my amazement, I found my thoughts drifting to ... Harry Potter. And it seemed to me that the popular children's series contained all the bizarre things that I had been sensing since my encounter with the locust. Voldemort and the Malfoys, with their mania for blue blood, represented a race that enslaved people with fear and "dark arts." Harry and Dumbledore's message about love triumphing over all, even death, matched my own revelations about trusting my heart. I had no way of knowing what its author, J.K. Rowling, intended when she wrote these characters, but I did know that the series existed and was hugely popular. It seemed to me that this would not be the case if she hadn't hit upon some truth that we all recognize, at least subconsciously.

The existence of these books seemed to indicate, quite blessedly, that I couldn't be *totally* off my rocker. Here was a cultural artifact that tangibly proved that the ideas racing through my mind were not simply products of my imagination—they were cultural memes that must, by virtue of their extreme popularity, be rooted in some kind of reality. I can't tell you how grateful I was for this touchstone. It sounds funny to me now—and probably dodgy logic to you!—but Harry Potter got me through that afternoon.

Later I learned about another story that seemed to relate to the experience I'd had. It is the story about the Buddha encountering Mara, the devil. As the Buddha sits meditating, he is assailed from all sides by the dreadful demon armies of "the Bad One." The Buddha faces the most repulsive monsters, with hanging tongues, bared fangs, eyes of burning coals, deformed bodies, devils with the heads of ferocious beasts. At first he struggles to maintain his composure, but eventually he finds equanimity. He indicates this inner peace by pointing one hand up to the sky and one hand down to the ground, a gesture meant to suggest that our place, as humans, is between heaven and earth. It also signifies the heart, which occupies the exact middle position between those two spheres. In the heart, we find the ability to discern.

All outside may be a-jumble but, if we are clear in our heart and follow our heart's guidance, we will not be led astray.

Although I had skirted the precipice of mental instability, I was still quite freaked out by the time Aaron came home. I tried to explain what happened to me, even telling him about the locust and the ETs. He looked quite worried, and that frightened me even more. He asked me to walk outside with him to get some fresh air, but the dusky light was the opposite of soothing. If ETs existed, then who was I to say that vampires didn't exist? And werewolves? And all the other shadow figures that populate our collective nightmares? (A few years later, once the "Twilight" series became immensely popular, I heard Bella exclaim the same thing I was thinking at that time in my life and took it as a sign that our collective comprehension about the world is indeed changing.) I knew that my heart was true, but outside myself, I had zero grasp about what was real and what wasn't anymore.

When we got inside, Aaron told me I had to calm down. I knew he was right, I just didn't know how to accomplish it. Everything I'd ever been told seemed untrue. At the same time, I didn't want to believe the alternate reality that I was perceiving. I was utterly terrified. I slept fitfully that night, with unpleasant dreams.

CHAPTER 8

Getting By with a Little Help

The next two days were difficult. When I checked with the *I Ching,* it counseled me to sit tight and meditate. This gave me some comfort; it felt as if someone were watching over me. Even so, I was in a fragile state. My head continued to buzz with doubts, amazing revelations, and fearsome thoughts. Invisible extraterrestrials, vampires, and werewolves seemed to be pressing in all around me while my mind cruelly played the overdone soundtrack to a bad horror movie.

At the same time, I didn't want to fall back into an unconscious state. As terrified as I was of the unseen beings, I didn't want to forget about or ignore their existence, either. I was like Neo in *The Matrix,* waking up to a hard bunk and cold gruel, but finding at least some comfort in finally seeing the truth about the world.

Like him, I also felt newborn, with all a newborn's purity and fragility. Interactions with people could be overwhelming, especially if the conversation wasn't truthful or connective. Television was particularly difficult. Its advertising and depictions of violence seemed garish and damaging. It made me heartsick to think of the way most people plug themselves into it as a soporific.

My first day back to school after what had happened to me— what I then simply thought of as my name-change explosion—was nerve-wracking. My head was still spinning, to the point of making me feel dizzy. And I was giddy, but not in a good way. In Chinese medicine, there is a pattern called "Heart Fire" that is characterized by difficulty sleeping, palpitations, and too much laughing (nervous laughter, in my case), all of which I had. I tried to stay in the back of the room and be as inconspicuous as possible, but even so, one of my dearest friends, Dana, could tell something was up with me. Since I knew she was interested in spiritual matters, I spilled the beans to her.

"Something amazing has happened to me—," I began.

Before I could get any further, she turned her big, astonished blue eyes to me and said, "Oh my god—I know what you're going to say. Me, too!"

Quite miraculously, Dana had experienced the same revelations about the nature of identity and the distinction between the egoic personality and the soul, at nearly the same time as I had. This seemed extraordinary to me, though I knew that Dana had been increasingly focused on meditation and various other esoteric practices since she began dating a yogi who lived in an ashram. As she pursued her spiritual path, the understanding of herself beyond ego had simply opened up for her one day, perhaps with much less trauma than I'd experienced because she was with someone who could contextualize what was happening to her.

I can't possibly express the amount of gratitude I felt to have someone with whom to share what I eventually came to understand was the awakening process. Dana became a very important touchstone for me and continues to be to this day. She also answered—in a profoundly abundant way—the humble request I'd made of the universe to provide study buddies to help me get through school, though little did I know what that would mean when I asked for it! Is it possible that Dana and I awoke at roughly the same time precisely because we were egging each other on, perhaps on some vibrational level? This seems likely, since it's the very reason that spiritual communities come together—to support and encourage each other. The principle is the same whether it happens in the context of a monastery or your yoga circle, family, or group of friends, a fact that Oprah Winfrey built on brilliantly when she and Eckhart Tolle co-led their "New Earth" classes on awakening.

Although Dana and another friend of the spiritual bent, KD, understood about my awakening, they couldn't comprehend my intense fear of extraterrestrials. To my surprise, they both believed in ETs and had no quibbles with my revelations; they just didn't understand why it would bother me so much. I was flabbergasted by their reactions, unable to comprehend how they could possibly know about this and not be terrified.

Stella: "Do you mean that you're perfectly happy to be a human coppertop?"

KD: "Ha ha ha, coppertop! That's funny!"

Stella: "It's not mine. Switch says it to Neo in *The Matrix*."

KD: "Coppertop … ha ha ha!"

Stella: "And it's not funny. It's twisted!"

KD: "You're not a coppertop anymore!"

Stella: "Thank god."

KD: "So don't worry about it!"

Stella: "But I was being feasted upon! By an invisible parasite!"

KD: "But you're not anymore! Don't worry about it!"

For her part, Dana suggested that I connect with a woman she had just met, a woman who claimed to be an ET, or at least an ET embodiment, whatever that means. Her name was Lisa Renee; Dana had just gone with her boyfriend to a talk that she had given. Thanks but no thanks, I told her. The last thing I wanted was to shake hands with an ET, even a beautiful Santa Monica version of one!

I did, at Dana's request, talk to one of the teachers at our school who was a well-respected Daoist. Not knowing how else to approach the subject, I asked point-blank what he thought about ETs. He looked at me suspiciously and asked me who was asking. When I said I was just trying to figure out for myself whether or not they existed, he seemed to relax a little bit and said, "Oh, they're definitely here."

Suffice it to say that this information did not stop my head from whirling.

Perhaps a week after my run-in with the locust, Aaron was still trying to calm me down. One night he suggested that we watch a movie. I tried to explain to him how much abhorrence I felt for depictions of violence and cruelty, but he prevailed and turned on *V for Vendetta,* a movie directed by the Wachowski brothers.

Despite its dark colors and somber mood, that movie was the perfect choice because its central theme is the awakening process. Natalie Portman plays the main character, Evey, who lives in a state of fear perpetuated by a government that controls its population through media manipulation and by orchestrating events of mass hysteria. Eventually Evey gets thrown in prison, where she is tortured and terrified until she overcomes her fear of death. At that point, she is released from what turns out was not a jail, but the shadowy V's methodology for helping her to awaken. Together Evey and V go on to help their fellow countrymen throw off the bonds of fear.

Since I could easily apply the metaphor about Evey's "death" to the annihilation of both my given and chosen names, watching this movie gave me proof that I wasn't alone, that others out there knew about the awakening process. Furthermore, it seemed uncanny that the first movie I would view after awakening would be about that very subject. Once again, my heart flooded with gratitude for what seemed to be the incredible care that someone or something was taking with me. There may be negative extraterrestrials but, I was also persuaded, they weren't the only ones out there. As the credits rolled, I cast around the still-dark room to see if I could sense any particular presence. What I felt was an incredible amount of love wrapping all around. It was a turning point for me in terms of feeling safe once again in the world.

Watching *V for Vendetta* also underscored the suspicion I had, as with Harry Potter, that the architecture of awakening is built into many popular stories. The more I explored that idea, the more I found to support it. *The Matrix* is, obviously, the leader in this class, but there are others, too. *The Kingdom of Heaven,* directed by Ridley Scott, counteracts ideas about the racial and cultural superiority of one religion over another. *The Golden Compass* depicts children leading the charge toward enlightenment. *Kung Fu Panda,* the Dreamworks flick, is about a boy who learns that wisdom is sourced from within. *Iron Man* is about a regular man with a superhero heart. For a more *avant garde* take on the topic, see any of Alejandro Jodorowsky's movies, but especially *The Sacred Mountain.* All these films shine a light on some aspect of awakened thinking.

As more and more movies with enlightened themes emerge and are embraced, the argument that we as a whole are becoming more awake gains credence. Perhaps this is the very purpose of story. We can't absorb the "whole truth" or all that unconscious juice straight up because it's simply too powerful and the ego too resistant. Stories may give us digestible pieces in a palatable form and, collectively, provide the tools to advance our consciousness. When we do awaken, they carry the threads that help us make sense of the journey we've just completed.

Of course, I'm referring to my awakening as if I knew that's what it was at the time, but I patently did not. It was only after more reading and learning that I put together what had happened to me with what people in spiritual traditions call "awakening," which describes a religious opening to a sacred dimension. One very helpful work on this topic was *The Emerald Tablet* by Dennis William Hauck, but it didn't come to me until after I was in private practice and one of my favorite clients brought me a copy. Perhaps it is important to have awakening experiences within an uncontextualized arena so that there is no doubt about authorship on top of all the other doubts that arise. Or perhaps it is simply that the ego is usually too strong to allow awakening experiences to arise when there is foreknowledge of the process.

That said, by awakening outside a grounded spiritual tradition, I was very much adrift at this time, grasping at anything that could help me make sense of what I was going through. Therefore other people's roadmaps became important to me. They were my first indicators that others knew what was happening to me and/or that we were having a similar experience—and this made me feel much less alone.

Meanwhile, at home, Aaron was growing increasingly frustrated with the state I was in. His confusion was matched by the difficulty I had in explaining what had happened to me. My words were like ghosts; they seemed to be missing a dimension. If I said, "I understand now that I'm not my name," he just shook his head and tried to stop himself from blurting out, "Well, duh!" There was always this slippery piece about my experience that I never felt I could communicate fully.

In another stroke of pure synchronicity, Aaron came upon a story about reptilians in the book he was reading at the time, Michael Harner's *The Way of the Shaman*. In it, Harner tells about exploring plant medicine in South America. After one particularly intense experience, he started perceiving a frightening reptilian creature that kept claiming to be in control of things, including Harner. Unable to shake his fears about this, Harner finally tells his teacher, the old village shaman, about the experiences he is having with this negative being. His teacher looks at him, laughs, and says, "Oh, don't listen to that guy. He's always saying that!"

Once he read that, Aaron seemed to feel a little more at ease about my experience. Behind a charming anecdote was an important lesson from the old shaman, who was basically saying, "Whether you believe it's an alien, a psychotropic hallucination, or an overactive imagination, negative energy is negative energy. Are you just going to buy into it?" When I later discovered David Icke's work, my own reaction was similar: We don't have to be ignorant about the forces at play on the planet, but neither do we have to pay the pesky, malignant, or sinister ones unnecessary heed.

On the subject of extraterrestrials Aaron said, "I can't prove it one way or another," but the story gave him a context for what was happening to me and helped him to see that I wasn't alone in what I was going through, especially among those on a spiritual path. I'm sure this eased his mind as to the sanity of his wife! It was another situation in which I felt watched over, as it seemed uncanny that Aaron would hit upon the exact passage we both needed at that time.

Others weren't so sure. Some of my oldest friends began a whisper campaign about me. One college buddy began telling friends that I had gone off my rocker. Her source was my blog. In the entry after my awakening experience I confessed that, in writing the previous post, something "had broken in me." While I didn't mention my ET revelations, it must have been clear that my sanity was somewhat precarious when I suddenly curtailed my posts.

On the one hand, I liked the idea of exploring these intense experiences I was having in the public domain, where they might help someone else coming to the same realizations. On the other hand, I didn't want to become unemployable due to revelations that I couldn't be sure I would own in the future. I was still very much grappling with the question of my sanity and whether or not my realizations were trustworthy.

Seeing that I was still struggling, KD suggested I see an acupuncturist in town named Dr. Mikio Sankey. Known for developing acupuncture patterns based on Sacred Geometry, he might, she believed, help me feel a little bit more grounded. I didn't know what sacred geometry was or how it might help me, but I was willing to see anybody, as long as they weren't an extraterrestrial! As luck or something else would have it, I was able to get in to see him quickly, despite the fact that his waiting list is usually at least two months.

Dr. Sankey's office is reached through a sunlit garden. Devoutly spiritual, meditating daily and cleansing constantly, he pads around his office in bare feet, dressed all in white, a Japanese American with a California surfer's vibe. He claims to have discovered his Esoteric

Acupuncture patterns with help from Djwhal Khul, the Tibetan master made famous by Alice Bailey. I liked him immediately.

Dr. Sankey doesn't do an intake by asking questions but by looking at the aura. He squinted at me and described the various colors of my energetic field and places where my qi was "leaking." I had no way to verify what he was seeing, a fact that didn't bother me one bit, since I had mainly come for answers—and those were spilling forth as Dr. Sankey, knowing I was an acupuncture student, nattered on about his acupuncture style.

First off, he told me that it was based on Kabbalah and its numerological system. Immediately I felt the synchronicities clicking into place. I thought it was extraordinary that I would stumble into a form of acupuncture based on the same system I had used to choose my name. Second, I learned that Dr. Sankey agreed that there were extraterrestrials, though he wasn't verbose on the subject. One thing he did say was that he was quite sure that all the monks in Dharamsala, where the Tibetan government in exile has its headquarters, talked among themselves about their experiences with what he called "little green men." The reason the monks didn't share their observations with outsiders, he said, was because they knew that people would only think they were crazy.

As Dr. Sankey's needles started to work, I began to feel floaty and calm, very close to a dream state. But then he added one more thing about extraterrestrials that set me on edge. He said that he had had a patient come into his office one day unaware that, in another dimension, an extraterrestrial was controlling her. Dr. Sankey described seeing a collar around the woman's neck attached to a leash. Holding the leash was a reptilian who hissed ferociously at him, saying, "She's mine!"

Suffice it to say that my floaty feeling dissipated, and when Dr. Sankey left the room ostensibly to let me rest, I did nothing of the sort. When he returned and asked if I was okay, I confessed that I was frightened, exceedingly so. He nodded as if he knew this would happen and assured me that I was just releasing fear. To encourage the process, he advised me to take a hot shower before bed and let the hot water run down the backs of my legs, where the kidney channel runs. Because the kidney channel is associated with fear, he claimed that this practice would help me release that emotion.

Dr. Sankey's guidance worked—on more than one level. When the terror started coming on again that night, I got in the shower and the hot water did, indeed, wash away my fear. But even more effective was Dr. Sankey's matter-of-fact manner. He seemed to know all about the spiritual process I was undergoing and take it in stride. When I got into bed after the shower, I had no trouble drifting off. I've since advised my own clients transitioning into new levels of awareness to treat themselves to hot showers before bed and they've reported similarly soothing results.

My friend KD made another suggestion during this time that proved to be a great help. A sporty gal with a ready laugh, she urged me to pursue the question of how my fear of extraterrestrials might be serving me. This question is based on an assumption about the world—that the things that show up for you must in some way be helpful, even if it's not immediately obvious how that could be. It's a provocative idea, especially if you don't like the world you're living in, but I found it useful because it encouraged me to take responsibility for my life. I chewed on that question for a couple of days before the answer hit me: More than anything, those negative extraterrestrials were showing me the extent of the fear I was carrying around on a daily basis.

Obviously, the reptilian bogeymen were scary in and of themselves. But once I thought about it, I realized that the largest part of the fear I'd been feeling since first seeing that locust wasn't about the threat of extraterrestrials. Rather, I was terrified that people might think I was crazy if they knew I was having encounters with them. This is understandable, given how much scorn can be heaped upon anyone reporting unusual, unexplainable, or transpersonal experiences or ideas, but it disappointed me to see how much I was affected by it. My father's concerns about our family's appearances to the outside world had become more deeply embedded in me than I realized. For as long as I could remember, I'd been walking around in a subtle terror about other people's opinions, hoping they didn't think I was ugly, or fat, or stupid. The fact that I was none of those things didn't matter one way or another; I was obsessing about it nearly all the time without fully realizing it.

Another huge reason the negative extraterrestrials spooked me was because they made me feel powerless. I couldn't exactly repel them with guns or fists or even loud words—they were disembodied and invisible, not to mention potentially imaginary! I finally decided that none of these concerns mattered. The only thing that mattered was my own relationship with fear and whether or not I indulged it. I decided to look at those times when I felt fear as an opportunity to shift into gratitude. In this way, I began to see the negative ETs as teachers, even getting to the point of thanking them for their lessons.

For instance, I might be sitting in my chair and suddenly feel another presence in the room. At this point, everything was freaking me out, even if the presence wasn't particularly negative. A cat could walk by on the deck outside and send me into shivers. But instead of losing it, I began to bow, sometimes internally but sometimes literally, to the presence or cat—to the fear, really. I would thank it for help in perceiving where my fear lay and then calmly ask it to leave. At first it took a lot of courage to do this with any sort of equanimity, but I got better at it with practice. Over time, my fear dissipated to the point that, these days, when I feel the presence of anything remotely menacing, I simply stand my ground and gently reaffirm the sovereignty of my personal space the same way I might remind a toddler not to tug at my hair.

Later, after I started learning about shamanism, I discovered that this respectful and compassionate way of dealing with negative entities is an important methodology for releasing them. In Alberto Villoldo's Four Winds Society shamanic training program, students are taught to use this diplomatic attitude, along with crystals, to release negative entities from the body. Here, the negative influence isn't necessarily seen as extraterrestrials, but perhaps as a habit, an ancestral pattern, sickness, emotional resonance, etcetera. The core belief—that we have choices—is the same. And the methodology—similar to what Carl Jung and his followers might call "Active Imagination"—is a powerful one.

Jung considered the practice of Active Imagination a potent path to self-development. In it, one actively engages the entities that come into consciousness, typically through direct dialogue. You hear what they have to say, engage them in debate, and find some way to come to terms. Jungian analyst Robert A. Johnson sees it as a "dialogue with genuine interior parts of ourselves," where "we confront the powerful personalities who live inside us at the unconscious level." James Hillman (another Jungian), who further developed the concept and practice of archetypal psychology, offers a broader take: "It's letting the figures that arrive on their own speak on their own. They may or may not be internal. Where they come from is, as far as I understand it, not your business." Concerned about how the scientific community would react, Jung initially kept his interactions with ancient prophets and mystics via Active Imagination to himself, but later revealed his methodologies and credited his most important breakthroughs to this practice. Whether we see them as ETs, energies, or unconscious personalities, the point is that they have something to offer us if we make the effort to engage with them, even if that interaction is limited to boundary-setting.

At first, because I was so scared, it was difficult for me to distinguish between negative entities and helpful ones. Over time, however, I noticed that negative beings carry conflict with them, almost as if they arrive on clouds of intense radio or TV static that cause one to question, question, question what the heart knows. Resisting those egoic inner voices can feel intense, like weathering hurricane-force winds without any shelter. During those times, it's helpful to remember that truth is undeniable: You'll know which way to turn, or what to say or do next, or whom to trust when it's obvious, when there are no questions. Positive entities/spirits/influences will always resonate inside with a big, undeniable "Yes!"

Intertwined with the concepts of personal sovereignty and boundaries is the use of permission. In the clinic, one of my most beloved advisors, Yvonne Farrell, DAOM, LAc, was adamant on the subject: We simply weren't to work on any level without obtaining permission from the person we were interacting with. Physically, this meant communicating clearly before touching someone and waiting for them to respond positively. She insisted that we apply the same courtesy when working on more energetic or psychospiritual levels. When we don't respect each other's boundaries and personal sovereignty in this way, we invite others (be they colleagues, spirits, extraterrestrials, or even self-sabotaging aspects of our own personality) to do the same to us. Thus integrity becomes a way to create a world built on mutual respect, in alignment with the Golden Rule. To this day, I believe that it is my job to stay in integrity myself, as well as to remember to clearly give and get permission.

About three months after realizing that it truly did not matter what I called myself, and wanting to follow through on my name-change project nonetheless, I consulted the *I Ching* about whether or not I should go through with it. The response I got was this: "The movement from chaos to order is complete. The time is extremely favorable and you are likely to enjoy much success."

My name-change project had stirred up an amazing amount of chaos—more than I'd ever experienced. Without knowing what was in store for me, I stumbled into one of the most profound experiences of my life. But by the time I got the go-ahead to actually change my name, much of the turmoil was behind me. By holding steady in the face of fear and learning to bring up and integrate shadow elements, I'd made it through to the other side with my sanity (mostly) intact.

I can't know what would have happened if I hadn't followed the *I Ching*'s advice and waited to change my name. I suspect that I might have slipped into trying to be that persona I had subconsciously attached to "Stella Osorojos" instead of awakening to a nameless sense of myself. Or perhaps my awakened self would have found some other way to break through.

Either way, I was glad to have waited. In the still time I had confronted big demons and found a way to make peace with them. I had also strengthened my trust in the *I Ching*, a book that I later came to see as a profoundly beautiful spirit, one vested with the great task of speaking truth through its pages. To this day, I turn to the *I Ching* whenever I have a problem that could benefit from selfless guidance, and I recommend it to other people, too. Of course, the *I Ching* may not be for all people, but I do believe that someone or something that can function for you as an ego-check is an important tool for spiritual growth. Traditionally this has been a guru or teacher, but it could just as easily be the Tarot, a coca-leaf reading, your spouse, a spiritual study buddy, or any combination of these and other guides on the path.

Being finally at liberty to go to City Hall and accomplish my mission, I had no hesitation. In the cool hallways of LA's Stanley Mosk Courthouse, I submitted the necessary paperwork and, one month later, I returned with Aaron as my witness. In a drab courtroom, a young courthouse clerk asked me in a monotone why I was changing my name.

I said, "Because I want to."

She said, "You can't just change your name because you want to."

"What do you mean?"

"It has to be a reason, like you've gotten married or something."

"Are you serious?"

"Yeah. You can't just want to."

"Well, I am married.... "

"Okay," she said and stamped the paper.

Thank god I never had to tell her that my husband's last name was Sugarman—and that he had decided he wouldn't be changing his to Osorojos.

CHAPTER 9

Friends in Wild Places

Though Aaron had flirted with the idea of adopting a married name that we would share, he ultimately rejected the idea after feeling a sentimental upwelling toward his given name. While I understood his reasoning and supported his right to adopt whatever name he wanted, his decision left me feeling lonely, as if my best friend didn't want to play with me after all. That minor abandonment underscored the larger chasm between us on the child front.

Every time I broached the subject, Aaron assured me that he still didn't want kids, but I couldn't let it go, especially since, instead of being blithely unconcerned about the subject, Aaron slipped into a funk every time I brought it up. A visible black cloud would overtake his features and he would look like he was trying not to vomit. I couldn't help but believe that such a strong reaction indicated something worth uncovering, if only to dissipate its debilitating hold; though, truthfully, I also hoped that if he confronted whatever fears lay behind such powerful reactions they would disappear and his attitude about kids would magically transform.

I knew that I was likely grasping at straws, but I was hearing and witnessing stories about wonderful health transformations in my school's acupuncture clinic. We also began seeing a marriage therapist together, which led Aaron to delve into a Jungian approach to dream analysis that he found satisfying and that began to attune him to the mysteries of life. Seeing that he was willing to change gave me hope—and I desperately wanted to stay open to the possibility of a miracle, especially because so much else was right in our relationship.

As Aaron explored his dreams and we continued to share our meditation practice, we got an invitation to go on a spiritual retreat in Oaxaca. Dana, Dr. Farrell, and another dear friend from school, Eric, were arranging a trip that promised to be mind-blowing. The introductory meeting was a fire ceremony in Eric's Mar Vista backyard that started with everybody going around the circle talking about their feelings, something the old Aaron would have been thoroughly icked out by. I thought for sure Aaron would never agree to go, but to my delight he said, "What the heck? I've never done anything like it before...."

Before jetting off to Mexico, Dana suggested that we prepare by having a session with a friend of hers from college who had become a channel, a person who brings forth messages from beings in other dimensions. One famous example is Sylvia Brown. In this case, Dana was suggesting Natalie Gianelli, who channels Dr. James Martin Peebles, a spirit who had been a well-known author and lecturer on Spiritualism at the time of his death in 1922.

I had never been to anything like it before and was somewhat skeptical, but the idea intrigued me, especially after hearing about Natalie's introduction to channeling. After graduation, casting about for something to do, Natalie had herself gone to a group session where a woman was channeling Dr. Peebles. When Natalie asked him what he thought she might do for a living, he suggested that she start channeling him. She was in her early twenties at the time and loathed the idea of channeling if it meant she would no longer be able to go out for a glass of wine with her girlfriends. When Dr. Peebles assured her that she could set the terms for their interaction, including spending her free time with a straw in her wine glass if she wished, she agreed. That sounded like exactly the kind of channel I wanted to meet!

I arranged to have Natalie come to our house for the session and invited perhaps half a dozen friends to join. Time permitting, we would all get the opportunity to ask a question or two. When I consulted the *I Ching* about what to expect, it said that a great new friendship was beginning, one that would bring mutual benefit to both parties.

The session took place in my sunny living room. An unassuming thirty-something with an irreverent laugh, Natalie hunkered down on the floor in front of our giant couch. I had a front-row seat and was glad for it, since I wanted to watch exactly what happened when Dr. Peebles showed up. Frankly, I wanted to see if I could detect any BS!

After a few minutes of silence, a new energy began to animate Natalie's body. Speaking with a Scottish accent, Dr. Peebles began his "State of the Union," a general address that outlined his beliefs about what he calls "this school called 'Planet Earth,' where we are never the victims but always the creators," as well as more topical concerns. If I remember correctly, his great push at the time was to let us know that everything was a choice between love and fear, and that it was up to us to decide which way we would go.

As he spoke, I stared baldly. Natalie's eyes were closed, so if I was being rude, she didn't know it. I just couldn't take my eyes off her since, while it was clearly her body, it was obviously not her moving it. At one point I even fancied that I could see Dr. Peebles. In the middle of my staring, I suddenly realized that I was looking at an elderly gentleman with white hair wearing a suit. The second I realized this, however, the vision vanished. It makes me wonder what else I might perceive if I practiced looking with that intensity.

When it came time for me to ask a question, I started by first saying my name, calling myself "Stella."

"Stella!" Dr. Peebles exclaimed. "What a *beautiful* name!"

This got a great laugh from the crowd, because all my girlfriends knew that I'd recently changed my name, but Natalie did not; she only knew me as Stella.

Personally, I felt chagrined by Dr. Peebles' words. I figured he might know more about it than I did and was teasing me. A major shift had occurred in my psyche as a direct result of having changed my name, but I still didn't understand exactly what had happened to me. I asked for his take on my experience.

He said that, truthfully, it didn't matter what I called myself, but that he felt that my wanting to change my name was a desire to acknowledge the changes happening in me. He also said that he and his cohorts (whom he didn't specify) were very proud and grateful for the work that I was doing, especially in learning to love and honor myself more.

It struck me that he would place so much value in how I treated myself. For one thing, it certainly was true that I was trying to be kinder to myself. My meditation practice had trained my mind to be more aware of the fleeting thoughts that circled through, so I noticed how often they were self-deprecating. Seeing this, I had the opportunity to let them go. This was bringing me more and more peace, and I knew that this was the "work" to which Dr. Peebles was referring.

His words also made me think of our interconnectedness. Was he saying that, somehow, my increased love for myself was increasing the amount of love that he and others were able to experience? If so, that would be wonderful, but how did it work, exactly? My curiosity about so-called metaphysical matters was sparked.

Another important lesson that Dr. Peebles imparted he called "The Inner Child Meditation." He pointed out that whenever we felt out of sorts in any way, we weren't channeling the higher self but the inner child. In fact, most people on the planet were channeling their inner child all the time, he said, acting and behaving from a place of pain and hurt rather than one of consciousness and strength.

The way to address this, as with all conflicts, he suggested, was to give our inner children more love and attention. Specifically, he advised that we should check in with our inner child for one to three minutes every morning. This might happen immediately after waking up but before getting out of bed. He instructed us to lie back again, close our eyes, and see, in our mind's eye, our inner child. Notice what she (or he) is wearing, what age she is, and ask her what she has to say. While the inner child is talking, let her speak without interruption, without comment, and certainly without belittling her feelings. Then, once she has finished speaking, thank her for sharing and assure her that you're an adult now and you're going to take care of everything. That's it.

It took me some time to make a regular habit of doing this meditation, but I can honestly say that it has brought me more peace and calm, more release from fear, than any other practice I've done. At first, whenever I checked in with my inner child, I realized that she was hiding from me. No matter how much I called to her, she absolutely would not come into my view. I could almost hear her saying, "Hell no! Not after what you've done!" Of course, I didn't really know what I'd done, and after a while I felt like an idiot continuing to call for her, but I persisted.

After about six months she finally appeared, but she would always stay on the other side of the room, as far away from me as she could. Slowly, slowly, she started to come closer and to tell me a few things. Invariably, the tears would flow. And I would have to explain to Aaron that I was crying about something that happened twenty years ago but hadn't been integrated! Thankfully, Aaron didn't mind and, over time, some of my old shadows and crusty fears chipped away. These days when I check in with my inner child, she's more often egging me on to do something silly and fun than appearing to be scared about anything. Over the years, sessions with Dr. Peebles have helped me in many ways, but this first one may have been the most powerful.

After the session, Natalie seemed a little woozy, and we had to regale her with tales of our adventure, since she never remembers much about what is channeled through her. Among other things, she was genuinely surprised to learn that I had recently changed my name.

Our Oaxaca trip was similar to a lot of the self-help encounters that are offered at places like the Omega Institute and Esalen, except that it was led by our friends, which made it extra fun and meaningful. In between enjoying the beautiful beaches and refreshing Oaxacan surf, we did things that were meant to test our boundaries and self-conceptions—things a reasonable person wouldn't be terribly eager to do if they thought about it too much!

One such experience involved jumping off a cliff.

Into churning ocean.

In the dark.

Naked.

When it became clear what I was supposed to do, I was willing but not happy about it. Generally speaking, I don't like cold, or wet, or being scared. Go figure.

So I approached the edge of this cliff with reluctance. The night was chilly, the stars were twinkling in and out behind clouds, and I was miserable. The facilitators had made it clear that none of us *had* to go through with the task they'd set before us, but I didn't want to be the only loser who chickened out so, pushing my feelings out of the way, I jumped. The chaotic water came much sooner than expected, and plenty of it went straight up my nose. I sputtered to the surface feeling thoroughly resentful and ill-used, entirely as if I'd been pushed and hadn't freely jumped. I've come to realize that so-called spiritual work is often like this. We expect airy mystical experiences and get more mundane-seeming physical and emotional jolts instead. But by approaching these experiences with the right attitude, they work their magic nonetheless.

In this case, I swam to the shore and took myself off into a personal space. In the dark night, I started to examine what was coming up for me. What was this feeling of being pushed? Why did I feel unprepared so often? As I thought about it, I began to wonder if perhaps my feelings went back farther than the night's experience. Perhaps they went as far back as my birth, as I had been born prematurely. Perhaps certain stories I liked to tell myself—about "they made me do it" or "it's not my fault because I wasn't ready"—were expressions of this pattern.

I saw that every time something comes up in life that triggers feelings of inadequacy, fear, despair, anger, etc., it is a way for me to tell myself that something's not right—that, perhaps unconsciously, I'm holding a pattern of thinking that creates these incidents as validation for the thoughts themselves. When these occasions arise, I have two choices. The first is to wonder what I did wrong and feel victimized by it. The second is to recognize that I've felt this way before and that there might be a pattern here, a pattern that's trying to point itself out to me so that I can look at it, perhaps even change it. One could say that this is the real self trying to awaken the dreamer. One can also start to understand how powerfully the subconscious mind programs our daily life. That night, as I soothed the pain in my sinuses from the ocean's surge, I also took good care of my inner little girl.

Another significant Oaxaca experience came in a group exercise. Each person was asked to step into the middle of the circle and state a fear. We were then guided to see how each of our stories was limiting us. When my turn came, I described being scared of leaving Aaron behind as I moved forward in my spiritual growth and over our conflict about having a kid. But no matter how much my facilitator, Eric, questioned me and no matter how long I stood there feeling like a complete idiot with everybody staring at me, I couldn't make a breakthrough.

Finally Eric caught my eye and said, "Let's just do this. Let's just go."

For some reason, I knew what he was talking about. I knew we were going to "go" somewhere inside. Moving as if in a cloud, I shut my eyes and started to sink into my feet. When I felt my arms rise over my head without my conscious instruction, I was momentarily confused, so I opened my eyes for a split second to see what was going on. Through my eyelashes, I saw that Eric was moving in unison with me, almost as if we had become a vehicle of synchronized parts.

Not knowing what else to do, I closed my eyes again, determined to follow the energy where it might lead. My focus became deeply internal. All my attention was focused on the area below my belly button, the *Dan Tien*. At first I was aware of muscle and gut, but as I continued to focus down and in, and as the shape my knees and hands made seemed to augment the pressure downward, compressing my attention even more, what had been heavy suddenly became light. In my mind's eye, I emerged from all that density into deep space with every star in the universe winking at me. Black velvet twinkled all around. Then, in a split second, I understood that these stars weren't all around me, they were *inside* me. I contain the entire cosmos, just as surely as you do.

When I finally opened my eyes and was back under the palapa roof at our Oaxacan retreat, I didn't know what to make of this experience. It didn't seem related to the fear I had been expressing. Apparently Eric didn't know what to make of it either, because he took one look at me and shouted in bewildered excitement, "Who *are* you?!"

Who was I, indeed? It was not a question I had any idea how to answer at the time. Quite apart from my relationship with Aaron, a feeling was growing in me that who I was had something to do with those "friends" floating above my bed in Los Angeles, the ones I had sent away back at the beginning of all this craziness.

Aaron had equally powerful experiences on the Oaxaca trip. He's not sure when it happened, but at some point he started to know what I was referring to when I spoke about awakening. I'm paraphrasing, but he explained it something like this: "I used to think that enlightenment was something that didn't really happen to ordinary people, that it was mythological in some way, and now I see that it is, in fact, possible." I would add that I believe that not only is enlightenment possible, it should be understood to be a natural stage of human development, the same as growing your wisdom teeth.

When we got home, the whole world seemed different. I still didn't have a child, but I was no longer struggling alone with my spiritual path. I had good friends and a caring husband who were on the road with me. What's more, I'd developed a passion for laying open all the fears that might be holding me back.

Good thing, too, since more of those were in store for me.

CHAPTER 10

I Grow Wings

During the time that we were in Oaxaca one of the big topics of conversation was the Mayan emphasis on the year 2012. That was when one great cycle of measuring time ended and another began, according to the Mayan long-count calendar. Because the prophecies of other cultures such as the Hopi and Mormons, and even the book of Revelation point to this general time as one in which a great shift will occur, it's possible that 2012 signifies more than just turning the page on a twenty-five-thousand-year-plus calendar. Nobody really knew what any of the prophecies or specific dates meant, but there was much doomsday speculation.

I was intrigued by this talk, partly because I had seriously considered becoming a Mayan art history scholar in college. Nevertheless, I was so busy with my acupuncture school that I forgot about the subject once we returned from Mexico. Then, browsing the stacks one day at LA's great Bodhi Tree bookstore, I spotted the kelly-green cover on a book entitled *2012: The Return of Quetzalcoatl.* Even better, it was written by a friend.

I'd known Daniel Pinchbeck back in New York City, when I was an assistant editor at *Condé Nast Traveler.* He and Thom Beller were the cofounders of *Open City,* a literary journal known as much for their parties as their aspirations in letters. I used to go with a girlfriend and feel terribly out of place in the racy, chic crowd, except when I saw Daniel, with whom I felt strangely comfortable.

I was vaguely aware that Daniel's first book, *Breaking Open the Head,* about his experiences with iboga, the entheogenic medicine of the Gabon people of Africa, had made a splash, becoming a phenomenon with the "Burner" crowd, those interested in all things tribal, dreadlocks, tattoos, consciousness, and the Burning Man Festival, held every summer in Black Rock, Nevada. My friend with whom I used to attend the *Open City* parties had read *Breaking Open the Head* and informed me that, sad but true, Daniel had obviously gone crazy.

Well, if Daniel had gone crazy, then so had I, for much of what I found in *2012* mirrored my own experiences. Drawn along by some form of inner knowing, Daniel describes following signs, having revelations, and contacting other forms of consciousness. More than the particular journey that Daniel takes, I felt a kinship with the book's substance, with the types of connections that he was making, with the expansions he was feeling, with, in short, his awakening process. His book was a mirror to what was happening in my own head—and the fact that what had happened to him was happening to me at roughly the same time seemed to indicate that some grander movement was occurring to connect us and move us all concurrently. I felt deeply grateful for the perspective that Daniel's book gave me on my own experience.

After that, I began to read everything I could get my hands on regarding 2012 and the Maya. During this time I came across Teilhard de Chardin's concept of the noosphere. This French philosopher and Jesuit priest's theory (suppressed by the Church during his lifetime) holds that human consciousness evolves as one, together with that of the Earth and all her denizens. This matched my experience, as I had seen a whole group around me awaken at roughly the same time and knew, via Daniel's book, that others were experiencing the same thing.

My forays into the literature of consciousness also led me to

Charles Eisenstein's brilliant *The Ascent of Humanity.* He looks at the roots and results of the belief that we have long held that we are separate from one another and not parts of a greater whole. These ideas about separation are what allow us to go to war with each other, to hoard, to hate. So many of these behaviors are written off as "human nature," but Eisenstein argues that even if that was once the case, it can no longer be. Multiple crises are converging, he suggests, that will spur us to see beyond separation to unity consciousness, though it may not look like what we think.

> For many people, the convergence of crises has already happened, propelling them, like the hippies or Taoist Immortals, into a release of controlled, bounded, separate conceptions of self, away from the technologies of separation, and toward new systems of money, education, technology, medicine, and language. In various ways, they withdraw from the apparatus of the Machine. When crises converge, life as usual no longer makes sense, opening the way for a rebirth, a spiritual transformation. Mystics throughout the ages have recognized that heaven is not some distant, separate realm located at the end of life and time, but rather is available always, interpenetrating ordinary existence. As Jesus said, "The Kingdom of the Father is in us and among us." This is the esoteric meaning Matthew Fox ascribes to the Second Coming: not a single definable event in objective time, but the sum total of all our temporally separated, fitful, but inexorable awakenings to Christ consciousness. What is special about our age is that the fulfillment of processes of separation on the collective level is causing this personal convergence of crises, and the subsequent awakening to a new sense of self, to happen to many people all at once.

While *Ascent* holds a special place in my heart, other books were helpful at the time too, including Eckhart Tolle's *The Power of Now* and *The New Earth,* which illustrate and point the way toward an awakened consciousness. In *The Great Turning,* David Korten argues that an awakened society should model itself upon sustainable structures. And in *Blessed Unrest,* Paul Hawken documents the surprising magnitude of the shift that's already occurring. My appetite for information led me to read countless others too, but these books in particular marked profound shifts in my understanding about what is happening to the world—and what could be coming.

Besides all the reading and studying I was doing, I began holding a meditation group at my house on Wednesday nights. Since meditation had played such a key role in my own awakening process, I felt that anything I could do to expose new people to the practice might help. That said, my initial group consisted of just a few neighbors, only one or two of whom showed up with any regularity.

One warm night Aaron and I and another friend were sitting on *zabutons* in our living room. The neighborhood was deliciously quiet. Just before I sank into a meditative state, I remembered to activate the acupuncture points that Dr. Sankey used in his Esoteric Acupuncture sessions with me, which I did simply by "tagging" them with my mind. I then silently asked for "The Wingmaker Frequency," as he had also instructed me to do. This was something I had done regularly since first seeing Dr. Sankey, and it generally produced a little buzz that allowed me to sink more deeply into meditation, but that was all. Not so this time.

About fifteen minutes into our sitting session, without warning, I heard a snapping sound and then felt a slap on my back that was so strong it pushed me forward off my cushion. Presumably thinking I'd fallen asleep and slipped off my cushion, my friend snickered. Aaron never moved.

Meanwhile, I couldn't believe what was happening. As I sat there, something seemed to shoot out of my shoulder blades. A corresponding vision of what it was blossomed in my mind's eye. First feathers, stiff and pure white, pushed out and then, all at once, giant wings sprouted out of my back. Within seconds, the weight of these enormous appendages was undeniable. Accompanying them was a whitish golden light that infused the area all around me. It was a marvelous, balloonlike feeling, as if I were being expanded from the inside. I was torn between wanting to open my eyes and try to figure out what the heck was going on and not wanting the feeling to dissipate if I did so. I wanted to balance right where I was for as long as I could.

Then the timer's chime rang and it was time for *kinhin*, or walking meditation. Since I was supposed to lead, I had no choice but to open my eyes. To my amazement, the miraculous sensation persisted. As I marched around my living room, the wings remained, enormous and weighty. I tried to catch Aaron's eye to see if he noticed anything, but he didn't seem to. Nor did my friend, who walked behind me and then settled down for our next round of sitting as if nothing were different.

I kept waiting for the feeling to leave, but it never did. All through the next meditation session and during the conversation afterward with my friend, I could feel this miracle on my back, as if I were at a costume party that only I knew about. I came close to asking my friend if she could see anything but couldn't bring myself to actually utter the words, "Uh, does anybody see wings sprouting out of my back?"

When my friend finally left, I turned to Aaron and point-blank asked him if I seemed any different. He said that I looked "kind of bright," but nothing out of the ordinary.

When I explained what my experience had been—and still was— he simply said, "Cool!" and looked impressed, a pretty good indicator of the amount of ambiguity we'd begun allowing into our lives about what was possible. I was relieved that he didn't try to shut me down or deny what I was feeling and marveled at how utterly unflappable he was, not to mention incapable of being jealous.

If the roles had been reversed, I'm sure I would have at least partly interpreted the fact that he'd had a big spiritual experience when I hadn't as a sign that there was something deficient in me. I definitely felt this way sometimes when Dana made spiritual breakthroughs. If she had a miraculous occurrence, it often triggered feelings of inadequacy and fears that I might be "left behind," or that I wasn't at the top of the class.

Of course, this entirely discounts the natural pace of spiritual unfoldment for each individual, but I think I was so trained by our school system and the emphasis my parents placed on getting good grades that I didn't know how to value myself if I wasn't being praised. For this was how I interpreted (at least subconsciously) experiences like this: as gifts that must be bestowed on the deserving. Now I see that this attitude misses the fact that experiences like this are neither good nor bad but contain aspects of both.

It certainly does seem true that for every amazing experience of connection there seems to be a corresponding letdown. This obviously happened to me after realizing the bliss that I wasn't my name, when I fell afterward into that great terror. A similar thing happened after the wings experience, where I walked around for a week feeling high and blessed—and so alive! Then the feeling of intense connection lessened and I collapsed into self-doubt. What was that? Did it really happen? What did it mean? Why didn't I know? What was I missing? I felt sure that I was inadequate to the gift.

Since this experience, I've gone through a few more cycles of spiritual unfoldment, and the process has become more familiar to me. Mythology scholar Joseph Campbell outlined these fits, starts, and reversals as part and parcel of the Hero's Journey, an archetype that can be found in good stories across all cultures because they reveal the deep truth about how we come into consciousness as human beings. Now I understand that there is likely to be a murky period to wade through at the end of each blissful cycle. The knowledge of this doesn't necessarily decrease the joy felt nor uplift the depressed bits, but it can help to know that these phases are natural—an aspect, perhaps, of the dualized world of form.

Edward Edinger, one of Jung's notable followers, believes that a period of either alienation or inflation naturally occurs after breakthroughs in awareness. This is how we learn and grow, how we become individuated. We realize that we are not who or what we thought we were, and either mourn that loss of identity or celebrate a new sense of expansion and power. The critical thing is to not get stuck in either of these reactions, as many people do, because over-attachment to the new persona will cut off the next round of development. For something new to be born, the old must die again and again, at least metaphorically.

The Buddhists would suggest that, as the human condition is filled with imperfect knowledge and misunderstanding, equanimity is called for during these (and all) types of experiences. They have a wonderful parable about a great master that illustrates this. I'll paraphrase it here because I like it so much:

There was a Zen master in a small town who generally reacted to things by saying, with the sort of twinkle that Zen masters are known for, "Is that so?" In that town, there was also a family with a beautiful daughter who had an illicit boyfriend. When she became pregnant by him, she told her parents that it was the master who had done the deed. When the family accused the master, he replied, "Is that so?" Later, when the baby was born, the family insisted that the master raise the child, telling him that it was his responsibility. The master took the child saying, "Is that so?" He raised the boy, growing to love him, but when the boy turned five the girl confessed her lie to her family. When they revealed the truth and asked for the boy back, the master handed over the child, saying, "Is that so?"

Well, needless to say, my equanimity was not at the level of this master's. I went to bed that night wondering if the "wings" would be there in the morning. I half-hoped they would—check out my angel wings!—and half-hoped they wouldn't. A part of me, the one that had always been made squeamish by all things New Agey, was mortified by the whole experience. There was the fact that my mother carried around little angel coins in her purse and wouldn't she just *love* the idea that her daughter, who spent much of her adolescence ridiculing those tchotchkes, might be turning into a believer. I needed some answers.

The day after that meditation experience, lo and behold, I ran into Dr. Sankey at my school. Not a part of the regular staff, he was there to discuss an elective the school had asked him to teach. By now somewhat used to mundane miracles, I felt it was no coincidence that he was there and only waited for him to finish speaking to a dean before accosting him.

"What was that Wingmaker Frequency?!" I blurted out. "I grew wings!"

Dr. Sankey shook his head, trying to figure out what I had just said. "What do you mean?" he asked, clearly perplexed.

I slowed down and told him the whole story. When I was done, his eyes quickly darted behind me and I saw them shift to the position he uses to better see energy. He said that he couldn't perceive any wings per se, but he could see that I was carrying a lot of energy on my back. I took this as endorsement.

This brings up, once again, questions about how to determine what is *real*. Should we trust someone because we are told that he or she is an expert? What about ten experts? Does the number of people who believe something determine truth, or only what is considered a social norm? How much does our belief create reality? The answers to these questions might be changing, especially as we incorporate new understandings about ourselves as interconnected beings. At the time, the only way I had of verifying Dr. Sankey's ability to see energy was my own experience—it certainly felt to me like there was a lot of energy on my back!

In part, I was persuaded to trust my own perceptions of things by the reading I was doing, reading that was showing me the limits of science, especially when practiced with measuring tools and beliefs that are blind to the full range of energetic and biomagnetic interactions that are occurring. People like the Dalai Lama and Sogyal Rinpoche, who wrote *The Tibetan Book of Living and Dying;* Gregg Braden, author of *The Divine Matrix;* and Lynn McTaggert, of *The Field* fame, were suggesting that my old views about the nature of the universe and what was possible in terms of human ability might be seriously outmoded. In this light, it didn't seem so weird that Dr. Sankey might be able to "see" energy, especially given his devotion to spiritual practice and service, which the above authors all agree plays a key role in learning how to work with the unified field. While I was grateful for Dr. Sankey's information, I was even more confused. If he couldn't tell me what this experience was about, then who would?

When I got home, I plugged every search term into the Internet that I could think of. The Web being what it is, I found some guy's site in New Zealand that was entirely devoted to the "Wingmaker Frequency" and the process of revealing and using these "wings." He included exercises meant to strengthen facility with one's own wings and suggested that wings are a natural aspect of the human form that only has to be revealed.

Despite containing some interesting information, the Wingmaker site was constructed in an opaque and overlapping fashion that made it easy to get lost and hard to get a handle on. I gathered that this was intentional on the part of its creator, who professed to want to keep this information esoteric. I sent the guy an email asking for more information but never heard back from him. I was left, once again, with a conundrum. On one hand, here was evidence that others out there were having the same sorts of experiences that I was having. On the other, how likely was this muddled, secretive, and somewhat obsessive approach to convince "normal" people of these things?

Next I turned to Dr. Peebles for an answer. In a session with channel Natalie Gianelli, I asked the good doctor what he made of my experience with wings. He had an interesting perspective: He said that I had been channeling, though I presumed that he was using the verb in a broader sense than the way Natalie channels, indicating that I was channeling energy and not necessarily some being's words. I thanked Dr. Peebles for his perspective, but I still wasn't quite satisfied. It was hard to put my finger on it, but somehow this didn't seem like the whole story.

In and of itself, this was a useful lesson. All the people we approach for help with understanding may have pieces for us, sometimes very important pieces. Nevertheless, the onus is on us to find our own truth and what resonates with our own heart.

Still searching for answers, I found myself drawn to the computer one sleepless night and ended up at the website of Lisa Renee, the woman whom Dana had met and who claimed to speak for a group of ETs. She had posted a description of her own awakening process and, as I read it, tears poured down my face.

Lisa's story was far more dramatic than my own, yet I felt a lot of resonance with her experience. After an intense kundalini experience, she went through a period of waking during the night to see recurring numbers flashing on her alarm clock, be it 1:11, 2:22, 3:33, 5:55 or whatever, over and over. This had also happened to me, and her site was the first place I heard of it occurring to anyone else. She also described an experience similar to the one I had when I woke up touching acupuncture points on my body.

Eventually Lisa discovered that she was "a walk-in hybrid and a Sirian Council Incarnate Member." I had no idea how to feel about that part of her story; I just knew that it felt profoundly good to learn about somebody else going through what I was going through. She hadn't written anything about growing wings, but I had a feeling she might know what that was all about, too. Though I was still nervous about meeting her, I shot off an email asking for an appointment.

CHAPTER 11

Meeting an Extraterrestrial— or Two

When the day came to meet Lisa Renee, it seemed like there was a lot of static in the air. My cell phone wasn't working well, so I couldn't confirm the appointment. There were no parking spaces and I had to circle the block several times. I didn't know exactly where we were supposed to meet and had to backtrack a few times to find her office, on the ground floor of offices constructed around a central courtyard. At every juncture I wondered if I shouldn't just give up and go home, but the difficulty in getting to see Lisa felt contrived, almost as if someone or something were trying to keep us apart. It all made me more determined to stick it out.

The first thing that Lisa said to me after arriving late to our appointment was "Did you notice the static? Somebody doesn't want us to meet!"

Lisa was tall and striking, but not so different than many of the other beautiful beings seen around Los Angeles. She sat me down in a chair opposite her and what followed was a "Quantum Analysis" treatment that fit in around a long, flowing conversation.

After exclaiming over "all the wonderful blue energy that you are carrying," she explained that she was an "Awakened Starseed" acting as an "Emissary for the Sirian High Council." According to her (and others), a "Starseed" is someone who has incarnated on Earth from another planet or star in order to help Earth transition into galactic consciousness. She said that we could all be considered Starseeds, since she believes that the entire human race came from other planets, and that the only difference between her and others was that she had perhaps arrived more recently. She believed that I was also a recent addition, as evidenced by my ability to sense invisible beings, as well as my sensitivity to sound and other forms of vibration.

While I didn't have an opinion one way or another about my being a Starseed, I was willing to give Lisa the benefit of the doubt regarding her own beliefs. For one thing, she didn't seem or feel crazy to me. She was well-spoken and had a light in her eye that, in Chinese medicine, is described as *shen* and indicates that one is both healthy and sane. Whatever she wanted to call herself, I liked her and didn't feel at all suspicious in her presence.

I trusted her so much, in fact, that I told her about the encounter I'd had just before grad school, when I woke up in midair and was rapidly touching points on my body, apparently locking or unlocking some sort of code. I'd never told anybody about that experience and was grateful for her reaction, which was simply to nod and listen. Once again, I regretted the fact that I'd asked whomever it was to leave. Yes, I had been scared, but I felt that if I had only held my emotions in check for a second longer, I might have been able to master my fear. And then ... well, who knows?

Lisa didn't have an opinion about that experience, but she did offer an explanation about my "wings." She said she believed that wings were part of the original human blueprint, which she described as once having had a twelve-strand DNA. She believed that we were being rehabilitated to this fuller expression of humanity with the help of all kinds of multidimensional beings in anticipation of the nearing shift in consciousness.

Later, writing about my "wings" experience for Reality Sandwich, I learned that Alberto Villoldo had reported something similar in his book *Shaman, Healer, Sage.* Talking about his teacher, he says, "Don Antonio used to say that *Homo sapiens* had perished, and that a new human, *Homo luminous,* is being born this very instant on our planet.... This means that we are that new human. We are the ones we've been waiting for."

While I was charmed by these ideas, I had no way of proving anything that Lisa had said. Over the next months and years, however, she did become a credible source of information for me as I started listening to the monthly talks she gives about all things related to what she calls "the ascension process." Month after month, I would link into her Q&A session and be astonished to hear her reporting exactly what had been going on with me in the time since the previous call. For instance, if I started getting dizzy spells or hip pain or a fluttery feeling in my spleen one month, then, almost invariably, she would talk about the appearance of dizzy spells or hip pain or that bizarre, otherwise unexplainable fluttery feeling as an "ascension symptom" during that month's call. Her reporting was so specific and unambiguous that it consistently broke down my natural resistance to the otherwise outlandish worldview she was describing. It all served to be more evidence in support of Teilhard de Chardin's noosphere concept that we are all linked and undergoing evolution in concert.

Fascinatingly, Lisa provides information about what these ascension symptoms signify on a planetary scale. Undergirding her concepts is the alchemical maxim, "As above, so below," which implies that the microcosm elucidates the macrocosm and vice versa. In other words, according to Lisa, our bodies manifest what's going on in the greater world. So when the Earth's fourth chakra, supposedly located in Egypt, is opening or the focus of conflict, then we may show symptoms in that region as well, be it palpitations or chest pain or what have you. As to the plausibility of this, I can only offer my own experiences, which seem to consistently and uncannily coincide with Lisa's messages. She has become an invaluable ally as I continue to try to figure out what the heck is happening to me—and all of us!

Despite the interesting perspective that Lisa offered regarding my wings, I still had questions. I continued to feel their invisible presence, though the intensity lessened. They became something that I carried around, something that I didn't necessarily notice until I tuned into them. I was still looking for answers.

Some months later, my friend Eric sent an email inviting me and Aaron to his backyard. A friend of his, a fellow shaman from Alberto Villoldo's Four Winds school, was unexpectedly in town, and Eric thought that a fire ceremony would be a perfect way to welcome him. We jumped in the car without a second thought. I felt full of excitement, sensing that something momentous was about to occur. When Eric's friend JT walked into Eric's living room, I knew I hadn't been mistaken. He had an electric energy about him.

JT sat down and said that after his Four Winds training, he had gone to a shamanic conference in Peru. There he had met a shaman whom he particularly respected, one of the so-called celestial shamans, or Altomisayok, who worked with the high-mountain angels.

I stopped him right there.

"Angels?" I asked.

"Yeah. They're called Apus. They're basically the spirits who inhabit the high mountains."

With shaking hands, I explained about my experience growing wings and asked what he might know about them.

Like Dr. Sankey, JT tilted his eyes in a way that let me know he was perceiving energy. After scanning my back, he said, "I can see that you have wings, but one of them is half-stuck. If you want, I can help you with that when we do the ceremony."

Well, knock me over with a wing feather! Here was someone who seemed to think it was commonplace for me to be asking about the energetic appendages growing out of my back, even if he did think they were lopsided. I knew right then and there that I was going to go to Peru with JT.

When I asked him to explain more, JT only said that wings are a normal aspect of the human energetic form, but that they are sometimes cut off or distorted by those forces who do not have our highest good at heart. I took this to be a reference to those negative ETs with whom I'd had my own experience.

The ceremony began a short while later. We gathered around the fire pit in Eric's backyard. As Eric kindled the flames, we talked quietly and laughed. Then JT ritually opened the space by honoring the four directions, and we began to sing. When the time was right, JT started moving around the circle, ministering to each person individually. I watched as he worked.

As he approached each person, he seemed to consult with some unseen guidance, nodding and grunting as if taking direction. Then his hands began to work, alternately "digging" or "cutting" or pulling at some etheric formation that only he could see. The extraordinary thing was each person's reaction, for JT's ministerings seemed to have outsized effects compared to his actions.

For instance, with one young woman, he seemed to be pulling some masklike thing off her face. He struggled with this task, trying over and over to get his fingers underneath whatever it was he was seeing. As JT worked, the young woman seemed almost bemused, as if she didn't quite believe his antics, though she was willing to sit still for them. But once he finally yanked the thing off, the young woman burst into tears, clearly startled by her own reaction.

When he came around to me, I was intrigued to see what he was going to do. I couldn't really think of anything that I needed. There was still some congestion in my right eye from my thyroid problem, but this had long since become a minor complaint and I didn't think of it much; it only flared up if I had a glass of wine or too much dairy. But to my surprise, he went straight to my eye and began raking out the mucky energy with his fingers. Even more surprising was the great relief I felt in that orbit for a problem that I'd long since learned to live with. My eye started tearing as the blockage released.

Then he went to work on my back, pulling out my wings and smoothing their feathers. When he was done, I felt the full energetic expression of them again, as after their first unfolding. After that, there was no question that JT held information with which I needed to connect, both for myself and as a way to help others.

After the ceremony, I told him we would be going with him to Peru.

CHAPTER 12

Angels, Apus, and Pachamamas

Cusco is an ancient city built on a steep hillside. In the old part of town, cobblestones line the streets and many of the massive walls bespeak the mind-boggling precision of Inca stone masons. Lights twinkle festively in the gentle mountains surrounding the main square, where, on weekends, couples walk together and make out on the benches.

We arrived from Lima in the morning, as all tourists do, since it is the only time of day that the weather is suitable for the tricky landing in the high valley of this sacred city. After a rendezvous with most of our party—JT, Dana, and a few other friends—we moved onto Paz y Luz, a healing retreat in Pisac. JT, who had never been there before, looked around and said that he could see why the American owner, Diane Dunn, had chosen this spot in which to settle. It lay in natural *seque* or ley line, he explained. I'd heard something about ley lines, but not much. By way of explanation, he pointed out the mountains on either side of her property; they were positioned as if talking to each other. It was easy to imagine that there was some energetic communication between them.

Later on, we gathered in a lovely glass gazebo in the center of the property for our first ceremony. Adolfo Tito Condori, the main shaman or *paqo* with whom JT worked, was most impressive. Struck by lightning when he was a child, he was subsequently struck three more times, the last time in his eye. This injury gives him an oth-erworldly look that is mitigated only by the amount that he laughs and jokes. Since the Q'ero understand lightning strikes to be a sign that one is destined for a spiritual role, there was no doubt that Adolfo had chosen the right profession!

Another shaman who made a good impression on me was an elderly woman named Doña Maria. Maybe four and a half feet tall, she often seemed to be drifting off, not really paying attention. Later I learned that during these times she was most likely commun-ing with elemental forces. When she seemed to be spacing out, she was usually having a conversation with a raincloud, influencing the weather for our benefit!

After introductions, JT led us all in a guided meditation/jour-ney. I'd done one of these before, with Eric, and I didn't like them, mostly because I didn't feel particularly good at them. While we were expected to follow along in our mind's eye, I had a hard time "seeing" anything or letting go, especially of feeling stupid.

The meditation started out with JT shaking his rattle. In a low voice, he instructed us to see ourselves on a mountainside. He told us to find a hole that opened into the ground. We were to enter the hole and follow the passageway deep inside. Next, we were sup-posed to come to an underground body of water, but, like I knew would happen, I was three steps behind, still outside the mountain, still wondering what the heck kind of hole I might be seeing in such a landscape.

As I fell further and further behind the meditation, I felt a wellspring of self-abuse rush up, full of messages about my being pathetic and noncreative. But rather than indulge these unhelpful feelings, I tried again. JT was by now leading the others off some-where I couldn't follow, so instead I found myself a hole in that mountainside and journeyed inward. Whenever I felt dumb, I just dug deeper. Eventually I sunk into a calmer state and, before I knew it, I was experiencing an actual vision. I saw myself being pregnant, but instead of a baby, I was carrying the world in my belly. I felt beautiful and large and peaceful. I knew that whether or not I ever carried a child, I was still birthing my life and somehow helping other people in the process.

When I came out of meditation, I thought about what this might mean and linked it to what I could now see clearly was happening in the world: A new time was being born and we were all helping to give it form. That's why we were all in Peru.

That glimpse of feeling out of my depth on the first night in Peru only intensified as the trip wore on. At each sacred spot we visited, we were guided to go inside and ask for increased spiritual connection. We also learned to make *despachos*, or offerings, as a way to petition for this connection and to clear heavy energies, or *hucha*. I doubted I was doing it right, and I was sure that even my thoughts were betraying me. Of course, this was the very *hucha* that I was seeking to release, but I couldn't help myself.

One of the main areas where my doubts congealed was around my relationship with Aaron. I still wanted a kid and he still didn't. He had made amazing strides in his spiritual growth and I found this attractive, but comparing him to the shamans around me, I also saw that he had a long way to go. Undoubtedly, it is not fair to compare anybody's spiritual growth to anybody else's, but I couldn't seem to shake the impression I had of him on that first trip as being stuck in fear. It seemed clear to me that if he would only let go of his fear of having a kid and his surety that doing so would bring nothing but ruin (to his sleep schedule, to his bank account, to his sex life), then he would make leaps in his spiritual growth. I had to make peace with the fact that he might never go there, or want to, and that I might have to leave him. One afternoon, at the edge of a cloud-darkened lake, I signaled my willingness to be guided on this matter by throwing the *mala* (a type of Buddhist "rosary") that Aaron and I had blessed during our wedding ceremony in Japan into the sacred waters beneath Apus Pitusiwray and Sawasiwray.

As I worked through my *hucha*, I was also learning about the Andean cosmology. Adolfo was a clear and patient teacher, one who took his responsibility with the utmost seriousness. He taught us that everything around us is alive, from the rocks and trees to the streams and mountains. What's more, he lived within this reality. As we walked along high-mountain passes, he might bend down, pick up a stone, and put it to his ear, gleaning information by listening to the living breath within that rock. The birds too were a great concern. He never missed an opportunity to interpret their movements in relation to us. For instance, as we drove to the mountains where we would be camping, a hawk swooped down in front of our bus, apparently leading our way. When Adolfo saw this, he whooped with excitement.

"This is a very good sign," he said.

Immersing ourselves in this world-view was somewhat familiar. In Oaxaca, we had done exercises in learning to read the signs around us, but here we were living it. Adolfo instructed us to stay constantly present, constantly asking for guidance, constantly listening.

One day we walked over a pass at nearly sixteen thousand feet, high enough that snow crunched under our feet and sunlight bounced into our eyes with fierce intensity. We were carrying stones toward a cairn at the top and, while we labored ever upward, feeling the lack of oxygen with each step, we were meant to infuse the stone with something for the mountain, a gift. I started thinking about my name and putting that into the stone.

As I approached the top, I heard a voice whisper into my ear, "Stella means starlight." I was quiet, so much in my thoughts that I nodded back to this and said aloud, "Oh, yeah." I thought I understood what this meant, which was that everything was light, including myself. Then I heard JT laugh, and when I looked up, I saw him looking down at the place from which I'd heard the voice emanate. Had he seen a being whispering to me? I wasn't sure if I believed this was possible. Or had he been laughing at me talking to myself? That thought made me color with shame and shoot him a decidedly unspiritual look. Divinity and *hucha*, all in the same labored breath. When I reached the top, I deposited my stone among the others already there, giving my name in service to whatever light it could carry for me and I for it. In return, I received a killer sunburn on the tip of my nose that spoke of the power inherent in these exchanges.

Peru was extraordinary for me from the perspective of lineage. The landscape gave me the most uncanny feeling, as if I'd been there before, though my family was from Colombia and not Peru. Nevertheless, the first time I stood in the presence of Peru's beautiful peaks, I thanked them for helping me to return. Later I would be told that perhaps I had been here before, but at the time I just wept with the strangest feeling of relief to be in their embrace "once again."

An even bigger lesson in exactly how mysterious and alive the world around us really is came when JT announced that we might be blessed with an Apu Ceremony, a ceremony in which the mountain spirits actually manifested.

Manifested? What?

Yes, manifested, JT assured everyone. The mountain spirits that we'd been praying to were actual beings who lived, most of the time, in another dimension. They could, however, manifest in our dimension when they chose. And Adolfo had cultivated the ability to call them in. If he tried, they might come for us.

I can't tell you how many conflicting thoughts this idea set off in my head. On one hand, I was beyond excited and, by this time, willing to believe that such a thing is possible. On the other hand, the idea that beings from other dimensions could fly through the walls, as JT described, sounded like science fiction, and I wondered if I was being conned, though there was nothing about Adolfo that suggested duplicity. Whereas my mind could concoct scenarios around one or two of the other shamans with whom we worked, in which we were the gringo fools who would believe any old New Age exoticism, there was no way to give credence to anything of the sort about Adolfo. In him I could see nothing but humility and pureness of heart.

JT prepared us for the ceremony by explaining a few things. First, it would be conducted in the darkness. This was for the protection of the Apus, who fully revealed themselves to humans only when they could be sure of their intentions. I was willing to accept this, though it did nothing to assuage my suspicious mind. JT also let us know that the Apus would be checking us out, gauging the amount of *hucha* we were carrying. We would make a better impression, he told us, by holding as much love in our hearts as possible. That I thought I could do, especially because, despite my doubts, I also felt exceedingly grateful for the opportunity to sit in on such an ancient and special ceremony, one that I had had no expectation of—certainly no knowledge of—before meeting JT and following him to Peru.

The ceremony took place in Aguas Calientes, the tourist town at the base of Machu Picchu. Adolfo's office occupied the front part of a building that had chickens in the back. The "chapel" was a windowless room constructed of concrete block. As we took our seats, my doubts gave way, partly because I couldn't see how anything could get in *without* flying through the walls. Also, the atmosphere in the room was distinctly churchlike, with an altar bearing images of saints at the front and plastic chairs lined up like pews.

Covering the altar were stones, crystals, candles, and each person's *mesa* or hand-woven bundle, which contained the *khuyas*, or sacred stones, representing the connections we were forging with the divine, be it Apus, Pachamamas (earth spirits), angels, elementals, or Amarus (underworld beings). Some of us had been building our *mesas* for years; others (like me) had received our first *khuyas* only the day before.

Finally, the doors were shut and everything went pitch black. Adolfo began praying and whistling, calling the Apus. After what could have been two minutes or ten, an amazing sound broke the silence: *Foomp, foomp, foomp, foomp,* the unmistakable sound of wings cutting through air.

One being seemed to arrive by penetrating the left wall, another from the right. A third came from behind the altar. Another seemed to fly up out of the ground. The ceiling had been tightly covered with a tarp and when a spirit penetrated from above, the twang of stretched plastic was discernable. I felt a wing pass by closely enough to feel its wind on my cheek.

Each Apu landed with a *thump* that shook the candlesticks. Then a clacking could be heard, what I later learned was likely the Apus blessing the *mesas.* Finally, an Apu spoke—and the noise was the most ridiculous thing I'd ever heard, a nasal vocalization that sounded like a 45 vinyl record revved up to 78 rpm. They announced their names, easily found on any Andean map: *Ausangate! Sawasiwray! Sacsayhuaman!* The Pachamamas were even more high-pitched: *Pacha Nusta! Pacha Virgen!*

Once I got used to their voices, I could better discern what they had to say, though it wasn't easy, since many spoke Q'ero or an archaic form of Spanish, both of which were beyond my proficiency. One of their main messages was about *ayni,* the Q'ero concept of reciprocity. The basic idea is that equal exchanges of energy are necessary to the sustainability and balance of the whole. Society itself will fall apart without *ayni.* In their world, this is often represented by the *despacho,* or ritual offering, which is given in exchange for otherworldly help, but it applies in interpersonal relationships as well. Great care is given to ensure that nobody takes too much and, just as important, nobody gives too much away.

The best part of the encounter came at the end of the ceremony, when the Apus asked us to sing for them, something they enjoy. We warmed up with a few campfire songs and then we broke out in a rollicking version of "This Little Light of Mine." By the end of the gospel song, our bodies and hearts were vibrating with all the love in that room.

When we emerged from the enclosed altar room perhaps an hour later, throngs were crowding the streets, making their way to a local festival in the town soccer stadium. We picked our way to a café where we could have hot chocolate and discuss what we had experienced. Some members of our group were shaking and skeptical; others joyous and laughing. I felt ecstatic. For one thing, I felt deeply moved to have been let into this ancient tradition at such a profoundly connected level. It made me wonder about the question that Eric asked of me—Who was I, indeed, to be so blessed?

Furthermore, I had had an encounter with beings who felt real, no matter what my rational mind had to say about it. That is not to say that I didn't continue to struggle with doubts and *hucha*, but the foundations of my worldview had significantly broadened. Things were not as I'd been taught to believe. Much more was available to us than I'd ever known.

Immediately after my spiritual awakening, I'd had an idea that this was true—that things were not as they seemed—but I still struggled with many doubts. It had taken more than sixteen months of questioning, digging, learning, and sifting for my initial suspicion to settle down into something more closely resembling conviction. I qualify here because I'm still engaged in learning and growing, and the very idea of conviction doesn't square well with the one thing that does seem to be true about the world, which is, as the Buddha says, that it's ever-changing. Nevertheless, this first experience with the Apus marked for me a great healing in the rift that ideas about separation cause. I've never felt quite so alone since.

Before we left Peru, there were two treats still in store. First, we visited Machu Picchu with JT. Since there were lots of other tourists there and we were all exhausted from our mountain trekking, we found a quiet spot after our tour and napped in the sun. For fun, JT started performing shamanic healings on everyone. When he got to the friend he'd brought along from Vermont, a young woman named Nina, he immediately started working on her back.

"Somebody's stapled her wings shut," he said as he began trying to pry the etheric bonds loose.

I was heartbroken by this idea, even thinking about it purely in a metaphorical sense. My fear of beings who would do this to others was gone, replaced simply by sadness. Why, indeed, can't we all just get along?

We wrapped up our trip by having individual coca-leaf readings performed by one of the shamans. When my turn came, the shaman told me that I would soon be moving to a small town, that I should return with JT to Peru, and that I had permission to write about the Apus, despite the general ban on talking about them with outsiders. At the time I had no intention of doing so, but look at me now!

Our way back home routed us through Bogotá. We had stopped there on the way to Peru so that my family members could meet Aaron since, due to our elopement, most of them still hadn't met him. Nor were they aware that I'd changed my name. My father had apparently been too embarrassed to relay the information, which I'd asked him to do.

I understood his concern—I didn't particularly want to tell them, either. Consisting of seven sisters, three brothers, and plenty of offspring, my father's family is formidable, and not just in size. All my aunts and uncles are highly educated, opinionated, and blow so much in the same direction that they practically form their own weather system. Growing up, my cousins were always telling me how lucky I was not to have the pressure of what amounted to seven mothers. I had always protested, saying how much I felt I was missing, but now I thought I might be able to see their point!

On our first stop, I had taken the weaselly way out and omitted telling them about my name change. I didn't particularly care what people called me, I reasoned, since I knew in my heart that it didn't matter. I was perfectly happy to continue answering to "Lali," as I'd always done.

Of course, those two days in Bogotá before Peru were at least equally and probably more stressful than just ripping off that Band-Aid and getting it over with. I spent a good part of each day hoping they didn't find my passport or that Aaron didn't slip and call me "Stella." A part of me knew I should just tell them, but every time I tried, shyness gripped my vocal cords in a stranglehold.

As we descended once again into El Dorado International, the nervousness returned about being "found out" regarding my name change. Try as I might to put this thought out of my mind, it kept popping up again. When I got to my aunt's apartment where we were staying, I threw the *I Ching* coins, asking whether or not I should come clean.

The answer was unequivocal: Integrity is very important for anyone, but especially those doing their best to follow a spiritual path. In other words, quit being a weasel! Because we would be in Colombia for less than twenty-four hours on the return trip, I had invited my family over for breakfast. I went to bed dreading the conversation that I knew would have to accompany the scrambled eggs I was planning for the morning.

When dawn came and my aunts and uncles began to pile in, I could be found ... hiding in the kitchen. Despite having already weathered so much friction about my name change back home, and despite my recent breakthroughs in Peru, I was terrified of my extended family's reaction. My only solution was to corner one of my cousins, tell her, and then ask her to tell everybody else!

Of course, my cousin didn't want to absorb the brunt, either. So, like a couple of eight-year-olds, we grabbed the one aunt we thought would at least understand if not support my name change. Ruth had not only been a hippie in her youth, but she regularly channeled guides and ascended masters and taught my cousins to do so, too. Her reaction to my name change?

"No! Don't tell anyone else, they won't understand! And change your name back immediately, Lali!"

Ruth's reaction was too funny for me. Whatever fear I had dissipated, and I simply marched out into the living room to face *la musica*. The collective reaction was possibly horrified, but overtly polite.

It felt good to come out of the name closet.

CHAPTER 13

La-La Woo-Woo

After that first trip to Peru, I struggled to reintegrate myself back into my life in Los Angeles. Descending in the plane toward LAX was heartbreaking. I couldn't believe that we found concrete and smog preferable to clean air and warm earth beneath our feet. All I wanted was to go back to those pristine mountains.

The first thing I did upon returning was to go for a hike in Griffith Park. Despite my still-burdensome *hucha*, I burst into tears at the sight of the San Gabriel Mountains. I knew they were alive. And not just theoretically alive, a projection of the unified field, but *living alive—beings*. I felt so held and so watched over and so much love all around that I had no choice but to relax and put doubts aside.

One aspect of my wanting to immediately return to Peru was, undoubtedly, spiritual competitiveness. Some part of me believed that the more I returned to Peru, the better, purer, cleaner I would become. In this way I might be able to help people and therefore have some worth in the world. Now I see that what I really needed was to learn to love myself better.

Much was changing on the home front. I graduated, passed my California and National boards, and started practicing acupuncture out of my house. I had some great clients and business was going well, but I wasn't sure that I wanted to stay in Los Angeles. After the shaman's prophecy about moving to a small town, I was drawn to the mountains. Aaron and I had always thought we might move to Santa Fe at some point, and I began to push for it. I hoped that once we got out of the city, Aaron might be more amenable to the idea of having kids, for which I was still eager and hopeful—though I knew that convincing Aaron to reverse his vasectomy would require a miracle.

Despite feeling called to move, every time I checked with *I Ching* it advised me that the time wasn't yet ripe. I'd long since learned to listen to the thing, so I sat tight and waited for the message to change. Meanwhile, the housing market, rocked by subprime mortgage fraud, began to sink.

During this time I contacted Daniel Pinchbeck and pitched him a story idea about the experience I'd had growing wings. "Homo Luminous: You with Wings" went up, attracted some interest, and was ultimately published in Reality Sandwich's first anthology, called *Towards 2012: Perspectives on the Next Age*. When the *New York Times* reviewed it, they called my piece "patchouli-scented and divinely inane." Being dismissed in this way was frustrating, not least because I had my own issues with essential-oil-and-ankle-bell aesthetics—and who doesn't regret having their own prejudices mirrored back at them?—but also because I loathe the facile undercutting of transpersonal experiences as New Age woo. Our lives are as large as our stories are allowed to be; without liminal stories, the ken of our psyches becomes small indeed. When such stories are finally allowed in our larger dialogues, it will mark a great healing in our collective consciousness.

I also wondered how the mainstream press could be apparently blind to what I saw as major news about our emerging consciousness. It seemed strange that so few "out there" were perceiving what I and my community knew was the story of our times: Namely, that we and our planet were undergoing a birth process of immense proportions—together. But nobody was talking about it that way on TV. Instead, they just kept reporting about each tsunami, earthquake, flood, oil spill, and revolution or uprising as if they were separate incidents, unconnected from each other and without correlative implication in our personal lives.

A major figure in my personal life at this time was a writer called Amely Greeven, the cousin of a friend from college. She and I had remarkably similar backgrounds: Ams had worked at *Vogue* while I was at *Traveler;* was half-Chilean while I was half-Colombian; as teenagers, we had both roamed around Newport, Rhode Island; later, nearly in tandem, we had developed interests in meditation (Amely had become a Vedic meditation teacher) and anything related to the Burner-shamanic-alchemical-Evolver movements. In order to provide a focal point for the energies we felt moving in the world— and to help them circulate more broadly, if only by providing a space where stories and ideas could be acknowledged and shared— Amely and I agreed to turn my meditation group into a salon and cohost it in my living room. In no time, we had scores of people joining us for fascinating discussions about the major changes we, at least, perceived to be happening in the world.

During one of these nights, a homeopath gave a demonstration about his craft, complete with videos of the near-miraculous changes in his clients. The next week, to our great surprise, one of those clients walked into our regular salon. While she had given permission for her images to be used in her therapist's presentations, she had no idea that she had been the star attraction in my living room only the week before. I was stunned by this coincidence—and doubly so when I learned that she was a Kabbalah teacher. After choosing a Kabbalah name, I had consciously chosen not to pursue any further exploration of Kabbalah, mainly because I didn't want to be yet another spiritual striver hoping for a glimpse of Madonna to go along with her hosannas. The fact that the universe would conspire to bypass this prideful squeamishness and arrange for a Kabbalah teacher to show up in my living room made me wonder what my relationship with this woman, Devandra, would become.

I liked Devandra almost immediately and was fascinated by the idea of exploring the tradition with which I already had a strange and wonderful connection. Furthermore, when I checked with the *I Ching,* it related that she would be "a wonderful teacher" for me.

One of the most helpful insights she ever offered me was about that initial experience with the locust/extraterrestrial. She suggested that the episode might have been what is known as *Halal Hapanui,* which she described as the space between states of consciousness. She explained that when we jump from one state to another, there is a period in between when we might "feel lost, ungrounded, untethered, confused, not knowing what to grab onto or hold up." It is a dangerous time when we could either break through or get lost in depression, anxiety and/or obsessive behavior.

It was comforting to learn of traditions with language for speaking about these types of experiences. It also suggests that there may be people out there who have entered *Halal Hapanui* but struggle to contextualize what they perceive. Some of them may be locked away in psychiatric institutions instead of where they really belong, which is in the hands of someone who knows how to navigate transpersonal states.

Meanwhile, Los Angeles was an exciting place to be for the spiritually inclined. In 2008, Reality Sandwich hosted a "2012 Conference" in Hollywood's James Little Theater. It was extraordinary to see a line around the block of awakened twenty- and thirty-somethings waiting for John Major Jenkins to talk about alchemy, Alberto Villoldo to discuss the shamanic perspective, Harjiwan Khalpa to extol us to be in our hearts, and for Daniel Pinchbeck to exclaim that he was "just trying to figure out what the heck is going on here!" Los Angeles was clearly a center of emergence for this movement.

Being in LA, I had great proximity to all sorts of spiritual teachers and holistic practitioners. Along with Devandra's Kabbalah treatments, I was receiving acupuncture weekly from one of the professors at the UCLA Center for East–West Medicine and continued to see Dr. Sankey on a regular basis. Perhaps the most amazing treatment I received was when JT returned to California for a spell and did a shamanic session on me out of a friend's house in Malibu.

It was one of those stunning California days as I drove down the coast with the water sparkling on the one side. JT invited me into a huge space overlooking a wide green lawn surrounded by mature oak trees. After we spent some time talking, he had me lie down on cushions in front of expansive glass doors. He called in the four directions then went to work. He shook his rattle over my body and held certain points on my neck. He did some journeying work, using Active Imagination to look inside the body.

Then JT said, "They want me to tell you that they are here for you."

He was looking at the trees outside as he said that, and when he looked back at me, I could see a twinkle in his eye that made him look about five years old. He whispered, "It's amazing—there are thousands of angels out there in the trees watching over you!"

With that, I let loose a cry that became racking sobs. I couldn't see anything there myself, but after my experience in Peru, I truly believed that the beings I'd felt around me my whole life really were there. It wasn't just my imagination—and it never had been! The relief I felt was enormous.

When I went home, I got straight into bed and spent the next two days crying. I realized that the source of so many tears was a deep-seated but ultimately untrue belief that I was alone. It was by far the most cathartic experience of my life.

Thinking about the experience later, I wondered what part JT played in unearthing or repairing this great wound in my psyche. It's easy to think that shamans or other types of healers can be powerful, or have some kind of otherworldly link, but what does *that* mean? With JT, I got the sense that it wasn't so much that his skills were better or his connection stronger than that of other people, but that he was carrying a vibration or vibratory range that simply shook more of me loose. In other words, he put my pain in a bigger context, understanding that I wasn't just lonely for company, or for a child, or for a companion who met me on all levels, but that I was lonely for it all, *plus* a sense of connected divinity, what you might call "god." By enlarging the net that I could fall back into, I could trust enough to let go.

While some healers work this way, holding our problems within a larger context for us, I also believe that their mere presence can be healing. *Witnessing* seems to be an important component of healing. By simply putting a hand on your scraped knee, your mother transmits something important about your own ability to self-correct. Certainly she is contributing love, but perhaps she is also acknowledging the boo-boo in a way that allows the completion of its own cycle. *Yes, you were hurt,* her touch imparts, *we can see that, contain it, and encourage the body to rebound back to health.* Without the presence of this compassionate act of witnessing, something festers. In this vein, we are all each other's healers.

As fate would have it, Aaron soon got the news that his company was going to be reorganized, folded into its giant corporate owner, its freedom greatly curtailed. This felt like the perfect opportunity to make a change, and when I checked again with the *I Ching* it agreed, saying I should put the house on the market. We did so the next day—and despite the market's increasingly rapid descent, our lovely Cheremoya Street home sold the very same day, even before it was officially listed. If I wasn't sure that the beings watching over me had something to do with our great good fortune, I was convinced when the buyer described having been "guided" to our place.

"I was going to put an offer on a house I didn't really want when something told me to look one last time on the realtor's website— and there was my house!" she said, sounding amazed. "Something just told me to look," she kept repeating. I had a pretty good idea that I knew what that *something* was.

Adolfo confirmed my suspicions on my second trip to Peru, which occurred two weeks before we closed the sale of our house.

When I told him of the seemingly miraculous pace of our deal, he checked in with his guides and then said, "Ah yes, that was Mount Shasta who arranged that for you." Thank you, Mount Shasta!

It was also, I was learning, a manifestation of my not being in fear about a sale. I had every reason to believe that it might take a long time for us to be able to move, but whenever pessimistic thoughts arose, I repeated a mantra—often simply "Love, fulfillment, joy, confidence, security, enthusiasm, balance, connection, and happiness!"—until the negative thoughts went away. The idea was that by vibrating at the frequency those words emit, I would attract more of that wavelength into my life. Even if that had nothing to do with a buyer showing up so quickly, it definitely kept me saner than I'm sure I would otherwise have been during the sale process.

Aaron did not accompany me on that second Peru trip. With the turmoil at his company and our house being under contract, he didn't think it prudent. I didn't mind his absence, especially because it meant that I got to bunk with an older woman whom I immediately adored. Her name was Jimena, and I think I learned as much from her as from the Apus on that trip.

When I met her, Jimena seemed to be as fully integrated in her powers as the shamans themselves. By that, I mean she was continually in conversation with the world around her. It was commonplace for her to interject a message from the trees or the mountains or a crystal into normal conversation. I think this annoyed some people in the group, not least because it seems so preposterous to our normal way of being and interacting, but I was intrigued and kept watching her, trying to figure out what she was doing and how.

I had a breakthrough with this one afternoon when we were asked to pair up and create a *despacho* together. Jimena and I chose to construct ours by a stream that flowed underneath one of the majestic faces of snow-covered Ausangate. As we worked in silence, I kept noticing the sound of the water gurgling. For a moment, I wondered if the stream were saying something to us, but then I pushed that thought away.

Later on, in our tent, Jimena and I were talking about my desire to have a child and she suddenly bit her lip, as if trying to stop herself from saying something. I begged her to tell me, and she finally relented, saying, "That stream that we were working by told me that you were going to have a boy and a girl, just like me!"

Obviously, this was a welcome disclosure, but it taught me more than to hope. I realized that I too had heard the stream imparting a message, but I'd chosen to ignore it and believe that it wasn't possible by denying what I had in fact heard. How many thoughts flit through our minds that we automatically dismiss but that might be bringing useful information? I made a deal with myself right there to listen more intently and be more open to the impossible.

When I got home, I found out that Aaron's company wanted to retain his services. He also had an offer to work for a friend of his at the BBC in London. There were appealing aspects to both options. If we stayed in our lovely house in LA, Aaron's new office would be much closer; he might be able to come home for lunch. The lure of a high-profile gig in London, with its proximity to friends and family in Switzerland, England, Belgium, and Paris, was obvious.

But somehow these carrots felt like glamorous traps, a test of our resolve. Our aspirations had turned inward and, though it offered nothing in the way of high-powered jobs and executive expense accounts, Santa Fe's great temptation was its simplicity and its opportunities for spiritual growth. We knew where our hearts were leading us.

CHAPTER 14

Mountains and Medicine in New Mexico

We arrived in Santa Fe in the spring of 2008. Our plan was to stash our belongings in a storage unit and perhaps travel a bit before deciding where to settle down. Should we move to Austin instead? What about Hawaii? In the end, though, that didn't happen. The house we were able to rent had a dry basement, big enough for all our stuff, and a location right in town. We spent the summer enjoying the copious charms of that walkable, art-filled city instead of moving about too much.

Santa Fe certainly can be captivating. There's a balanced tension in the softened geometric forms of its adobe houses, all set against amazing robin's-egg-blue skies, that energizes and calms all at once. It's the same on the area's hiking trails, which are sun-baked and harsh, spiked with quartz and mica—and covered with fresh-smelling, evergreen piñon, too. The mountain range that backs the small city captures this richness of opposites perfectly: The Sangre de Christo mountains are soft and gentle, yet named for the bloody hue that appears on the peaks at sunset. Spring, when hollyhocks push up from hard-packed mud, is pure heaven.

Though we had a sense of having moved to nirvana, we didn't necessarily know how we were going to make it work. Aaron had a severance package that would last us for about year; after that, we had to find some other source of income in a city that's notorious for drawing people and then spitting them back out when the reality of paying the rent in its quirky, insular economy hits. Again, we went into trust mode, presuming that we were there for a reason and, if not, we would understand where to go next once that door opened.

We did take one trip that summer. In June I got a call from a couple of school friends who had just moved to Denver. They thought we should meet midway between there and Santa Fe in a tiny Colorado town called Crestone. I'd never heard of Crestone, but when I looked it up on the Internet, I found out that it is a spiritual center that attracted a lot of Tibetans who felt that its energy is strikingly similar to what they left behind in the Himalaya.

Besides being the home of seven different Tibetan retreat centers, Crestone also supports a Soto Zen center, a Native American retreat center, a Carmelite monastery, a Japanese Shumei center, and three Hindu centers. Shamans are particularly attracted to the area, not least because of the Crestone Peaks, two 14,000-foot mountains that loom above town, as well as the proximity to Mt. Blanca, a mountain that has long been sacred to the Native Americans in the area. Shivers ran down my arms as I read.

On the first trip to Peru, JT had recounted a prophecy about "the eagle" and "the condor" coming together. In his telling, the "eagle" was North America, symbolized by the United States, and the "condor" was South America, especially Peru, which is so closely identified with that magnificent bird. To help this prophecy about reunion emerge, JT explained, many shamans had traveled to the United States to "wake up" the mountains there. By performing ceremonies and apologizing for many years of indifference, they had roused them, thus instigating the construction of an esoteric architecture needed for greater spiritual awareness for all. This had taken place, JT noted, in the Sangres, which ran from Santa Fe up into Colorado. It seemed likely to me that Crestone might have been the exact place, since it felt like the spiritual heart of the Sangres. I was intrigued that the offer of a jaunt to such a location would pop up seemingly out of nowhere. My unseen spiritual travel agents were doing an A+ job!

Crestone lies in the San Luis Valley, known as the Bloodless Valley to Native Americans who considered it too holy to have ever shed blood in it. About halfway there, some peaks at the northern end of the Sangre de Cristo range began dominating my attention. I couldn't take my eyes off them and, as with that burbling creek in Peru, I had the distinct impression that they had something to say to me. As we got closer, I realized that Crestone was located at their base and that we were headed right there. I knew I had been summoned for some reason, though I didn't yet know what.

My impression that we had been guided to Crestone was underscored when, after dropping our bags at our B&B, we went out to find our friends, who had left word that they had gone searching for one of the town's three *stupas,* a type of sacred Buddhist shrine. We didn't know which one they'd intended to visit, but we ventured out anyway, hoping to get lucky.

Lucky definitely happened, though we didn't meet up with our friends until evening. The first *stupa* we found was on the main road that connects all of Crestone's retreat centers. *Stupas* have tall spires supported by massive bases that one is meant to circumnavigate a certain number of times while praying or repeating mantras. As Aaron and I began to circle the *stupa,* the most amazing thing happened. Out of clear skies, perhaps a hundred tiny black birds suddenly descended all around us. They settled within a few feet of us and just watched. I immediately remembered Adolfo's advice that Apus often take the form of birds and felt deeply touched. I thanked them for their blessing, for it seemed patently obvious that that's what it was.

Just for a minute, stop to imagine how much I'd been changed by the events of the past years. Where I once might have perceived nothing but some random birds, here I was now seeing divinity in them. I've come to believe that spiritual development is like this: The outside events don't necessarily change, but one's perception of them does. Perhaps this is why it is so hard to study spiritual evolution:

trying to measure outside phenomena is the wrong tack when it's the internal environment that changes.

At the next *stupa,* another blessing took place, but this time in human form. As we circled the monument, a Tibetan monk descended from the parking lot with a group of perhaps four or five Americans. They began performing a ceremony and then invited us to join in. Just by being out in the world, open, stumbling into it, we received the second beautiful blessing of the day.

The third blessing was petitioned for by us the next morning in the form of a *despacho.* We wanted to hike up to Willow Lake to make one, but, as had become my habit, I first checked with the *I Ching* to see if such an offering would be welcome. It indicated that it would and that I should be "like a bride processing to the marriage altar."

I didn't know what this meant until we got up on the trail and then I felt it: the distinct sense that I was being scrutinized. It was as if the mountains themselves were checking me out. I tried to remain calm as we hiked up to 11,000 feet, but the sensation of being watched only intensified as we got higher. I wondered if I were being auditioned for something and, as at any job interview, I tried to be on my best behavior. In this case, that meant staying in a state of love, even as my awe of those powerful mountains grew.

The path was steep and then steeper. We passed a gorgeous valley waving with tall grasses and then climbed some more. Warmth and sun slowly gave way to chill and snow. We got near the top but couldn't make it all the way to the lake because the icy drifts were still too deep at that altitude. I felt as if the mountain were telling us that we were close enough.

When the time came to assemble the *despacho,* I worked quickly, wasting no time in assembling the necessary seeds, flowers, and candies since I didn't want to overstay my welcome. The vitality in those mountains was undeniable and I felt very respectful toward them. Later, when I checked in with the *I Ching* to see how we'd done, I got the message that "our gift was accepted."

I relate these messages from the *I Ching* in a very matter-of-fact way, but can you imagine what it is like to ask questions of a twenty-seven-hundred-year-old book and, again and again, have the answers be directly relevant to the question?

Soon after we returned to Santa Fe, a friend of ours who is a successful architect in town called up out of the blue. Friends of his had been trying to sell their house for months. "I don't know why I didn't think of this before," he said, "but my friends' house might be perfect for you...."

Was it ever. I got the phone number of the architect's friends and called them up. Within the first few sentences, the bells started dinging. When I asked the woman why she was selling, she said that her husband was from Rhode Island and they were moving back there.

Ding ding ding.

"Really? That's odd. I'm from Rhode Island," I said. "What did you do here in Santa Fe?"

"I am a travel writer."

Ding ding ding.

"Really? That's odd. I'm a travel writer! ... What's the address of the house?"

Without giving the actual address, let's just say that my numerological bells were ringing off the charts when she told me. I knew immediately that we'd found our house.

When we saw the place, my premonitions were confirmed. Not only was the house beautiful, it was just the right size for us and even had a guest studio with a separate entrance that would be perfect to use as a clinic space. Best of all, it sat on two acres at the base of the Sangres. It was as if the Apus themselves had chosen the spot for us—and perhaps had even auditioned us for it! We made an offer, numerologically connected to the street address and date we first visited the house and, naturally, it was immediately accepted with no haggling. Thank you, Crestone peaks!

Before the closing, I had a guilty crisis. I wondered if the place wasn't too grand for us and whether we deserved such abundance. I threw the *I Ching* coins to get a reading on this question and received the answer that the house "wasn't just for us." I hoped this meant that we would soon have a baby there but thought it might also refer to some of the plans we were envisioning.

Inspired by the sustainability and permaculture movements, we thought we might be able to transform our patch of desert into something lusher. Catching rainwater, applying mulch and mycorrhizae, and planting tree guilds (symbiotic collections of plant species) would be our means to this end. Once we did some work on the place, we hoped our friends would consider it a resource for retreats and reconnection with the Earth. It was exactly what we were hoping for ourselves, too.

Once we settled into our new home, we set to work on our plans and started to see transformation much more quickly than even we could imagine. We installed some rainwater catchment and, equally exciting, planted some fruit trees. I loved what I saw happening to the backyard.

If my external world was becoming more and more beautiful, my internal world was getting more and more interesting. After decompressing from Chinese medical school and not picking up a book for at least eight months, my love of learning sparked up again. I developed a keen taste for all things esoteric and read everything I could get my hands on, including Barbara Brennan's *Hands of Light,* all of Joshua David Stone's Ascension series, and Mikio Sankey's works on Esoteric Acupuncture. As soon as I finished one book, another on the exact topic of my interest would show up, sometimes seemingly out of nowhere.

I delighted in the uncanny sense I had that these texts were being sent to me, and I loved sharing the tidbits I was gleaning from my reading with my clients, who seemed to like coming to see me as much for the conversation as for the needles. I was only too happy to share what I was learning. At one point, when a client remarked about how much information I held, I joked that "My guides apparently know that if they want me to know something, all they have to do is get me the book on it."

Later on, in another session with Dr. Peebles, the grand spirit confirmed my suspicion when, answering some question I asked, he said, "We tease you a little bit, but your guides say that they'll be getting a book to you on that subject very soon." Suffice it to say that I'd never previously spoken to Natalie Gianelli or Dr. Peebles about my love of reading.

Another set of books that touched my heart was the Ringing Cedars series by Vladimir Megre. A Russian businessman who had come into contact with a descendant of a lost Vedic tradition known in the Siberian taiga, Megre authored nine books about his encounters and thereby launched a green movement in the former USSR that sought to obtain a two-and-a-half-acre plot of land for every citizen. Called "Kin's Domains," these plots were meant to restore no less than the sovereignty and self-sufficiency of human beings. I was moved by the fact that we had secured what amounted to a Kin's Domain for ourselves without realizing how crucial such a step could be. I felt as if, like Jumping Mouse, I'd landed in paradise.

Soon after moving into my house, I turned my attention to my clinic. I was especially interested in learning more about energy work. Back in grad school, I had seen a fellow student cup his hands over the needles after he'd put them in. When I asked him what he was doing, he said that he was performing Reiki, which I knew was a form of energetic transfer that often involved the use of symbols and "attunements."

The next time I had a patient, despite having no training, I followed my colleague's example: I put my hand over the needles and suddenly my hands started to move about by themselves. I had no idea what was happening, but it felt pretty good, so I kept doing it. Over time, I came to be more familiar with guiding energy in this way.

I also began to be aware that I could transmit other kinds of information. The first time this happened was in my school clinic. One of my patients was a dancer; I could glean that much from the build of her body. But before I could ask further questions, I found myself blurting out, "I see you have a connection with roses."

She looked at me, startled. I was startled too, because I had no idea where that sentence came from. When she said, "How did you know that?" I had to confess that I had no idea. She then confirmed that she did indeed love roses and kept them in her house all the time.

Over time, I became more and more familiar with the process of "knowing" things. An idea would pop into my head, just as it had with the stream in Peru. Instead of dismissing it, I would wait. If it lingered or kept popping up over and over, then I would venture to say something. Almost every time this happened, especially if I had no idea how this message could possibly relate, it turned out to be meaningful to my client.

In many traditions, it is understood that this way of knowing simply comes with spiritual growth. Jung might say that I was becoming more familiar with both the personal and collective unconscious. Personally, I link it with simply continuing to meditate, which seems to be a good way to deepen and refine the skill of listening.

Sometimes my "knowing" would seem to come from a particular relative of a client. Instead of a sentence or thought, I would feel a distinct presence. After waiting to see if this feeling persisted, a step that I considered crucial in order to ensure that I wasn't just indulging fantasies on the part of my ego that I could hear messages from the beyond, I would ask about the daughter or grandmother or whomever I felt. This was nearly always satisfying for my clients, as it was for me. I loved helping people make heart connections with their loved ones.

I also had an extraordinary experience with one of my own relatives, my father's father, my Abuelito. As I was setting up my treatment room, I began thinking about decorating with a photo of my grandfather, Manuel Antonio Chamorro. He had been a physician in Colombia while he lived, even acting as the Surgeon General for a time, according to my father. I had met him many times on trips to Colombia and, though I loved him, we didn't have a close relationship, mostly because his English was worse than my Spanish. Nevertheless, I couldn't stop thinking about his picture and finally asked my mother to have a copy made.

The first treatment I did after getting Abuelito's likeness framed and placed it in my treatment room, something unexpected happened. I had put needles in my client and was holding her feet, running energy through my hands into her body, when a feeling of weightiness anchored my palms down. Then I became aware of another sensation, this one shooting down my limbs, as if someone had come in through the back of my neck and had put my arms on like a shirt. I knew it was my Abuelito.

Since I didn't feel scared at all, I simply noticed as he went to work on my client. He seemed to be cleaning something out from her uterus, which I surmised because I could feel the corresponding sensations in my own belly. I knew he was done when my own sensations dissipated and my hands no longer felt anchored down. My client's response to this treatment was one of amazement, for she had felt the presence of my grandfather, too.

After that day, I was often aware of my grandfather beside me in my clinic. I love the fact that I feel closer to him now than I ever did when he was alive. Our relationship continues to grow, with his death—and our language barrier—being no obstacle to our magical work together.

CHAPTER 15

Starving for a Breakthrough

Despite the joy I was finding in my home and practice, I was struggling again on the relationship front. I had been sure that, once we were settled in a beautiful place with a beautiful garden, Aaron would see how spacious our lives could be and would show more interest in having a child. When he didn't, I experienced every emotion possible on the subject, from anger and rage to grief and sadness. I even felt relief. For although I didn't share this fact with Aaron, I did often feel as terrified of having a child as I longed for one. When friends wondered why I stayed with Aaron despite our being so at odds on such an important topic, I knew in my heart that this was no small part of the reason.

Another reason I stayed was that I was looking for—and believed in—miracles. Through my own studies as well as conversations with Dr. Peebles and various other teachers, I was learning just how powerful I was. With clear intention and perfect nonattachment, I could more and more frequently manifest the most amazing, if mundane, things.

For instance, shortly after setting up a beehive in my backyard, I decided I really should buy an EpiPen in case one of my clients ever had a bad sting. The adrenaline-filled injection systems that counteract the effects of severe anaphylactic reaction are usually obtained by prescription. As a doctor of Oriental medicine, I knew I could procure one, but I wasn't that familiar with the New Mexico laws and didn't really have a whole lot of time to figure it out. On a whim, I suggested out loud that the universe was going to have to get that for me if it was really in my best interest. Not being able to see how in the world such a strange and specific thing as an EpiPen was going to show up at my house without my doing something about it, I truly had no attachment to the outcome. I let it go.

To my utter astonishment, my houseguest walked into my living room the very next day holding an EpiPen and said, "You're a doctor. Do you need one of these things? I have more at home and I don't really want to pack it back in my suitcase." I had no idea that her allergies were severe enough to warrant such a device. I took the thing knowing that it was in truly having no attachment to the outcome that this tiny miracle was able to happen so quickly.

If this was possible with small things, why couldn't it happen with larger ones? Didn't couples sometimes get pregnant despite having had vasectomies? Or was I fooling myself, seeing miracles in pure coincidence and masking my fear of having a child behind a Virgin Mary quest gone mad?

Certainly, the friends who knew my thoughts told me to drop it and just find some way to convince Aaron to have his vasectomy reversed. But Dr. Peebles encouraged me, saying that things that seemed miraculous one hundred years ago were commonplace now. He suggested that I focus on asking for the emotions I associated with having a child in order to call in those vibrations and to decrease the amount of attachment I had on the subject. The fact that he was a spirit speaking through a medium did nothing to convince my increasingly worried girlfriends, but something rang so beautifully true in his advice, while something else seemed too horribly wrong in forcing Aaron to go under the knife against his wishes, that I elected to follow it.

I also frequently had crushing doubts about my chosen pathway, of course. How does one have a child by oneself, just by whispering into the wind? But I couldn't see any other way that respected both

Aaron and myself as sovereign individuals with the right to create and choose our own destinies. Yes, I could leave him, but I didn't want that, either. As tense as our relationship was over the question of whether or not to have a child, it was good on many other fronts. We had both refocused our lives around spiritual pursuits and we loved cheering and egging each other on as we shed more and more fear. This led, in the summer of 2009, to our doing a four-day wilderness fast.

Sponsored by the Upaya Zen Center, the wilderness fast took place at their refuge in the Truchas wilderness. Called Prajna, which means "wisdom," the retreat center could have easily been named "Natural Beauty." Think log cabins and wide-open fields surrounded by pristine forests, mountains, and streams. After a couple of days of meditation and other preparations, we were sent out with water, a tarp, and a sleeping bag and asked not to return for four days.

Aaron had done the program two years before and encountered a bear on that trip. Sure, the bear had ambled away without ill effect, but this adventure terrified me. Of course, that's why I had come—to face and clear fear.

I ventured out to a spot I had chosen in view of the peak of a mountain called Sheep's Head. For four days I slept, talked to my inner child (who thought this was the most fun thing I'd ever done), stared at the mountain, visited with the pines and squirrels ... and had horrific nightmares about tortured souls chained in dungeons. I also spent a fair amount of time thinking about ice cream, specifically Laloo's Goat's Milk Dulce de Leche. I was weak when I shuffled back to Prajna on the last day, but happy thinking that I was done with my ordeal—and that Aaron could no longer claim to have conquered a fear that I had not!

It was only when Aaron and I got back to our house that I realized that something deep had been stirred up by the fast. Despite having been quite blissful up at Prajna, we started fighting almost as soon as we got home. I picked the fight and it was about Aaron's failings as a man. Even as I made my accusations, I wondered why

I couldn't let it go, why I had to ruin what had been an amazing trip. But it didn't seem to matter how much perspective I had on my actions; I couldn't stop myself from ripping into him.

As I cried and accused, I was simultaneously steaming green beans on the stove for a late lunch. Soon I realized that there was no more water left in the pot and that I was burning the bottom of the pan into charred black goo. When I saw this, I told Aaron I was going to go outside to cool off. He nodded but didn't answer. I left him staring oddly at the burned pan and its unpleasant contents.

In bare feet, I made my way out to a spot on our land that felt special. A round clearing surrounded by piñon, it was cool and had a thick ground cover of pine needles. I lay down and asked the trees and the earth for help. Suddenly I felt a welling up of something within me. I wriggled around, trying to release whatever it was. I had the distinct impression that some sort of entity was struggling to emerge. Finally it seemed to slip out through my face, leaving the sense of having been a man, or a ghost of a man. Then I was calm, or at least as calm as anyone can be after such a bizarre incident! When I collected myself and ventured back into the house, I found Aaron gone, having left behind a note that said he didn't know when he would be back.

Dazed by what had happened to me in the clearing, I decided to take a bath with Epsom salts. Dr. Farrell had always talked about this being a particularly grounding remedy—and it definitely seemed as if more grounding was called for. I soaked until Aaron returned.

When he found me in the bathroom, Aaron sat by the side of the tub and listened as I told him what had happened to me. Then he told me an amazing story of his own. He said that when he saw the dark, burnt mess on the bottom of the pan, something told him not to touch it and to just get out of there. He had never had a feeling like that before, though he knew that I had, and he wondered if his increased connection wasn't the result of the wilderness fast. This alone was amazing for him.

Grabbing his bike, Aaron followed his feeling to the next mountain over. He knew there was a *stupa* on private land up there and, despite not knowing where it was, he *knew* he had to get there. Lacking directions was just the first obstacle. The neighbors, who liked to discourage traffic in the area, had installed a gate on the road and made sure there were no signs to the *stupa*. Abandoning his bike, Aaron hiked up the steep private road. When a car stopped to ask if he was lost, Aaron confessed that he was trying to reach the *stupa*.

"He was some archetypal old weathered dude," Aaron said, his eyes full of wonder. "He nodded, made direct eye contact, and told me how to get there. I never would have found it by myself. I was guided." There was more. He said, "I had this terrible sense of you being possessed—that the words you were saying were not your own. That the black stuff in the pot was something worse than burned food. And I somehow knew that visiting the *stupa* would protect me."

He returned bearing freshly picked wildflowers because, as he said, "Something told me to return with love, not fear or anger."

I don't know what it was that came out of my face, or what Aaron perceived to have blackened our pot, but I do know that after this incident something changed between us. The anger that I had learned how to control but nevertheless frequently felt toward Aaron no longer existed with the ferocious intensity that it previously had. That alone was worth giving up a year's supply of Laloo's!

Incidents like that taught me to hope. They gave me the palpable sense that Aaron and I were clearing karmic detritus. If we kept on peeling away layers of hurt and anger and fear, surely we would emerge transformed. At each stage, I watched to see how Aaron would reassemble the remaining pieces of himself, praying that a self-definition would sift up that could encompass enough love to hold a child.

In fact, Aaron did change. By 2009 he was open enough to allow that, while he still didn't want a child, he could see that I did and was willing to help. He offered to get his vasectomy reversed, though he wanted to wait a year to do so. While something nagged at my conscience about this offer—I didn't think it was ideal that Aaron should be entering into fatherhood as a favor to me, instead of as an enthusiastic participant—I put my qualms aside and accepted. My cousin, who is a successful couples' therapist in Geneva, had advised me not to insist that Aaron approach fatherhood in only one manner, but instead to be grateful for the open door that Aaron was actually presenting me. This had felt like very good advice, so I went on with my life, looking forward to the day, one year hence, that Aaron would go through with his surgery.

CHAPTER 16

Arcturus by Way of Peru

While I waited for Aaron to get his vasectomy reversed, life went on. I resumed my esoteric probings and continued seeing clients. I continued meditating, continued working on releasing fear, continued hoping that I would get miraculously pregnant so that Aaron didn't have to go through with his dreaded surgery. In some ways, I was functioning at a relatively high level, and in other ways I was just waiting, waiting for my life to begin.

The good Dr. Peebles was a great comfort at this time. He kept reminding me that although things were not one hundred percent with Aaron, he was doing a very good job of holding space for our mutual transformation. He noted that we were absolutely each other's best teachers. To me, that felt patently true.

In one session with the Doctor at this time, I asked a question that I thought might have an interesting answer. I knew that Lisa Renee believed that many of those connected with her were what she called "Starseeds." I was willing to believe that many humans had origins beyond the planet, not least because many tribal peoples with long oral histories, such as the Dogon and the Hopi, held this conviction. My awakening experience had also taught me to distrust the commonly accepted stories about our origins. That said, I had no opinion one way or another about whether I myself was a Starseed and generally preferred to simply refrain from thinking too much about it. But that day, out of nothing more than curiosity, I asked Dr. Peebles, "Who am I?"

This was his answer: "Well, of course, my dear, you are god ... You are the air you breathe, the sun that shines, you are god. But, also my dear, you have had very many lifetimes on Arcturus."

Arcturus? Huh? I'd never heard of such a star. I filed this information away in my memory banks and didn't think of it again for some months.

Then, bored one day, I googled "Arcturus." The Wikipedia page on the subject told me that it was a red star in the Bootes constellation named after a bear. A red star named after a bear? A red bear? ... Osorojos? Stella Osorojos? Well, that was bizarrely point-blank. Maybe the good doctor *had* been onto something ... Hmm....

Next I googled "Arcturians" and came across some books written by David K. Miller. A psychologist in Sedona, Miller claimed to be in contact with the Arcturians and, on his website, he talked a little about them. He said they were beings who occupied the fifth dimension and were interested in healing through acupuncture, sacred geometry, and Kabbalah. He also said that they worked a lot with a blue light.

Wait a minute! Wasn't I an acupuncturist who used sacred geometry in her treatments and had changed my name to a Kabbalah-inspired one? Hadn't Lisa Renee exclaimed over the "blue light" she saw all around me? Suddenly I remembered that long-ago afternoon down by the pond, when Camellia named me a star sister. Was it possible that she was more correct than she could have known?

It was all too weird!

I called Miller up immediately and booked a session to "speak" with an Arcturian myself.

Unlike Natalie Gianelli, who is a "full-body channel," Miller channeled by relaying the messages he was receiving in his own voice and words. I found this to be a lot less exciting than Natalie's method, but the content was intriguing.

My first question was about my possible Arcturian past. The spirit that Miller had contacted, supposedly an Arcturian named Julionno, said that not only had I been an Arcturian in previous lifetimes, but that I had also been a Peruvian shaman who had had contact with Arcturians. During that lifetime, he said, I had discovered how to implant the desire to change my name into this lifetime and had done so with the intention that it would awaken me.

Obviously I had no way of verifying Miller's messages other than my experiences. It truly had been the strangest feeling of undertow that drew me to change my name, a feeling that had been so compelling that it caused me to weather disapproval from all quarters. And though I had journeyed to many parts of the world as a travel writer, I had never had such an uncanny feeling of having previously been somewhere before as I felt on my first trip to Peru. There was something that clicked in Julionno's notions about my past lifetimes—and the fact that the name I had chosen resonated so strongly with Arcturus was fascinating—but I tabled this information as an interesting distraction. Even if it were all true, there didn't seem to be any point in making a big deal about it. I didn't want to style myself as an extraterrestrial, no matter how glamorous a model Lisa Renee presented.

I did, however, take this information as a good excuse to follow my ever-present travel bug back to Peru again! This time Aaron joined, which made me happy in part because I hoped that the shamans there might somehow affect his desire to have a child.

In February 2010, we found ourselves once again in Cusco. Just before our arrival, mudslides had wreaked havoc in Peru's Sacred Valley, stranding tourists atop Machu Picchu and devastating many of the towns outside Cusco. Because of the danger, we were not able to visit the high mountains. Instead we did most of our work with Adolfo in Urubamba and Pomacanchi, praying, meditating, making *despachos,* and clearing *hucha.*

A small town on a lake by the same name, Pomacanchi has a sign on its outskirts that declares it the "Ecotourism Capital of

Peru." The town is less untouched than the countryside, but lovely nonetheless. A whitewashed collection of adobe houses marches out from a central square. Cows and goats wander the streets. All around, Andean peaks bask in their own magnificence.

Just behind the center of town is a mountain called Pichupucara, topped by a cross. We climbed it one day, chewing coca leaves as we went. At the top, Adolfo encouraged us to pray and then speak to the surrounding mountains. We were to share anything from our heart and ask for their blessings.

As I stood up and felt the presence of those great beings, I felt at a loss for words. Instead of coherence, tears began to pour down my face. After a while I began to whisper. I told them that I didn't know for sure, but that I may have been there before. I told them that if this were the case—and even if not—then I was standing here again out of my great love for them. I promised to do my best to respect and transmit their teachings. As I spoke, a steady breeze dried my face.

Whether or not I'd been there in a previous lifetime, the change that was evident in me from my first Peru trip to now was extraordinary. Instead of feeling goofy and awkward, I was connecting with the Earth around me as if it were my family. I felt as if I were exactly where I was meant to be. I knew I was seen and heard and loved in return only for seeing and hearing and loving. I was home in some way that didn't need proof. It felt really good.

Up until that point, I had participated in the rituals that our Peruvian teachers set before us with an alternating flow of emotions that could include embarrassment, joy, squeamishness, disconnection, or wonder, but rarely real connection. That didn't come at first—and I'll venture to guess that it won't for most Westerners. We're simply too unfamiliar with ritual space; it makes us feel like fakes. But this doesn't have to be our only response. With time, rituals can become something more vital, something that connects us with sacred parts of ourselves that would otherwise go hungry.

The next day, we were ready to receive a *karpai,* a new level of initiation in the Altomisayok tradition. We traveled to a vicuña preserve (these animals are similar to llamas) outside Cusco for our ceremony. There, by a lake where geese paddled, the shamans began reading coca leaves, asking the Apus which *karpai* each of us should receive and whether or not we should receive one at all.

As we went around the circle, I was moved by how spot-on each reading seemed for each person. When Aaron's turn came, Adolfo explained that he was told to do a *karpai* that would balance Aaron's masculine and feminine aspects. Adolfo was confused by this since that type of *karpai* was not in his lineage. He said he didn't know where it might lead Aaron, spiritually speaking, but that he would perform it, since the Apus were clearly asking for it. I felt that my intuition about the importance of his coming to Peru had been correct. I also realized how strange it must be for Adolfo to be interfacing with Westerners who bring with them traces of many different spiritual paths. His own learning curve in this time of transition seems no less steep than it is for the rest of us.

I went last. As I waited for the shamans to do their work, the geese began honking loudly and splashing. After throwing the coca, Adolfo looked up at me, concerned.

"The Apus say that you have lost your previous two *karpais*. They say that you have given them away."

I knew immediately what they were talking about, though I'd never spoken a word of it to anyone. Once, when doing energy work on a client, I had felt something dislodge in my chest and fly away. I lurched after it, instinctively knowing that something valuable had left, but whatever it was, it had gone. Not knowing what to do and not having anyone to ask about it in the United States, I had put the experience out of my mind. To hear the Apus name it now as something so precious was devastating to me. At least I was able to take some comfort in the fact that I knew that the only mistake I'd made was to be energetically ignorant and perhaps over-generous with my clients. When Adolfo asked if I had tried to perform a *karpai* on somebody, I shook my head truthfully and explained.

Again Adolfo threw the leaves. He said that my path had been very difficult and he didn't understand why. He could see that I had a strong spiritual connection, but he couldn't really account for it. Why did the Apus and elements work with me on such a deep level, which he believed they did, if I wasn't yet prepared to handle their energy?

It was then that I ventured to tell Adolfo what the Arcturian channel had told me—that perhaps I had worked in this lineage before, that perhaps my connection was from a previous lifetime. For the first time, I felt like it really could be true. I was a Starseed. I had been a Peruvian. I had implanted my name and awoken myself. And here I was, clueless but returned.

As I spoke, the shaman who trained with Adolfo, a twinkly Q'ero called Victor, nodded, saying he understood. For his part, Adolfo looked at me with tears in his eyes and said, "I know it has been hard for you. It will get easier now."

In the end, I received the two *karpais* that I had previously lost, plus another one. As Adolfo promised, it made me feel better, like a hole in my heart had been repaired. Despite what I'd previously thought, I knew I would return again someday to Peru; it was in my blood.

CHAPTER 17

The Truth about My Marriage

Finally the time came for Aaron to have his vasectomy reversed. I called around and got a recommendation in Albuquerque for a male fertility specialist. Aaron was clearly uncomfortable with the whole topic, but he tried to play along. Whenever I brought up the subject, he tensed and looked pale, but he didn't protest so I pressed on, trying to trust that he wouldn't have offered to go through with the surgery if he hadn't somehow found a way to make peace with it.

A few days before our appointment in Albuquerque, disaster struck. A nagging injury Aaron had acquired downward-dogging in yoga class suddenly developed into crippling back pain. Sitting was excruciating, and walking or standing wasn't much better. At first Aaron tried to downplay his discomfort, but soon he was spending hours lying flat or crawling around the floor in agony.

Seeing him that way broke something in me. I knew that, on some level, his back pain stemmed from his deep reluctance to undergo the surgery and that, in trying to accommodate me, he was literally prostrating himself. What I was inflicting on Aaron was torture, plain and simple. At that moment I knew that although we loved each other, we were hurting each other by staying together. I knew we would break up, though I had no idea how I would ever find the courage to leave him.

Anyway, there were other things to focus on, such as getting Aaron to rejoin the land of the mobile. I buried the truth about my marriage under a frenzy of care, arranging bodywork and acupuncture and energy healing sessions in an effort to help him feel better. Gradually he began to emerge from his cocoon of pain, though what seemed to give him the most relief wasn't any particular modality but time and my telling him to forget the surgery, that he was off the hook on that score as far as I was concerned. He didn't probe my change of heart too deeply and I didn't offer much beyond pointing out that if his back was any indication, it was clear to me that he really didn't want to have a child.

I busied myself in other ways, too. I tutored kids after school in reading and writing; I taught physiology and pathophysiology at a local massage school; I studied ortho-bionomy, an osteopathy-inspired form of bodywork; and I cofounded the Santa Fe Time Bank, an alternative currency system that allows members to exchange "Time Dollars" with each other as a way to reestablish community ties. Time Banks or Hour Exchanges, as they're also called, have the potential to help people transition during this time of great economic and social change. I poured tons of energy and time into it, as did a slew of other Santa Feans. Within a year of launching, we signed up more than one hundred Time Bankers—and membership kept mushrooming from there.

I also turned ever more strongly toward my spiritual life. I continued to meditate; I continued to chat with Dr. Peebles; I continued to consult the *I Ching*. The messages I consistently got back were simply to continue asking for the emotions I wanted to experience—connection, divinity, joy, love, partnership, beauty—and to let the universe take care of the rest. I did this with increasing surrender since I had no other choice; I no longer had any hope that Aaron might change his mind about having children.

After Aaron got better, I got worse. I knew what I had to do but couldn't find the heart to do it. In protest, my body began to shut down. It started with simple depression, but I was soon having all of the worst thyroid symptoms again. Phlegm clogged my vocal cords, my eyesight got blurry on one side, and I started having horrific panic attacks.

The first one came on a night during which I was alone in the house. Aaron was away on business in Los Angeles when I woke up from a dead sleep with my heart racing. Convinced that I was dying, I ran through my options. I could go to the emergency room, call up one of my girlfriends, or just give in and let go. Strangely enough, I felt fine about dying. Aaron knew I loved him; so did my sister and dearest girlfriends. I lay down and tried to sleep, pretty sure I wouldn't make it to morning.

The next day I was surprisingly still alive, though somewhat groggy. But things just devolved from there. Soon my panic attacks were accompanied by violent retching and diarrhea that could come on at any moment and last for hours. When I had my thyroid levels checked, they were officially out of range and I was diagnosed as having autoimmune thyroiditis, a.k.a. Grave's disease. I knew that my emotional state was contributing to my worsening health, but I still didn't know how to leave Aaron.

He did begin to notice that something was seriously wrong with me and, seeing that I was at a loss to care for myself, he adopted the lead role as family doctor. After doing some research on the Internet, he decided that we should try a gluten-free diet. He was finding a lot of people reporting that cutting out all wheat, oats, barley, spelt, and soy solved most if not all of their thyroid symptoms. I agreed to give it a try, and within three days I started to feel a marked improvement; within six weeks I felt better than I could remember. Since changing my diet I haven't had any panic attacks, and my thyroid levels are inching back toward normal.

In the traditional Chinese medicine paradigm, there is no concept of autoimmunity. The body is assumed to be intelligent and would never attack itself; there must be some kind of pathogen. In the case of autoimmune diseases, usually that pathogen is characterized as a "damp-heat" or "wind" or a combination of the two, since "damp-heat" is seen in symptoms such as diarrhea, the relative heat in the skin of a fibromyalgia sufferer, and a variety of phlegmy manifestations; while "wind" is understood to be at the root of, say, the neurological complications in multiple sclerosis, as well as any itching or rashes, such as in lupus erythematosis.

In my case, the "damp-heat/wind pathogen" isn't a virus or bacteria but seems to be gluten, something I can more or less easily avoid. Presuming that my symptoms continue to ameliorate, it could be argued that what I have isn't *autoimmune* but *allergic* thyroid disease, though the pathway to the clinical manifestations is, admittedly, mediated through my body's own defense mechanisms. That semantic distinction could be important to make for the benefit of patients. When someone is told that his or her body is simply attacking itself, there is very little recourse but to feel betrayed at the deepest level, and the temptation to give up is strong. In contrast, someone who understands that health can be vastly improved by the small choices made every day to be kind to oneself is far more likely to embrace his or her own self-empowerment. Helping one another step into this mode of being is, I believe, the highest calling of any health-care worker—indeed, of any human being. As Albert Schweitzer said, "Each patient carries his own doctor inside him … We are at our best when we give the doctor who resides in each patient the chance to go to work."

Because it's just too good an opportunity to pass up, I have to interject an anecdote here for dog lovers. During this whole time that I was sick and getting sicker, so was my dog, Baloo. A miniature Australian shepherd, he was having terrible digestive problems, waking us up four or five times a night needing to rush outside with diarrhea—poor thing! Knowing that our animals sometimes communicate with us through their illnesses, I wondered what he was trying to tell me. Since it was his large intestine that was acting up, I wondered if he was trying to convey something about letting go? Or emotional incontinence? Or maybe, in forcing us to go sleepless, he was trying to point out to Aaron that, baby or not, he couldn't count on life being gentle all the time. Lo and behold, when I switched Baloo to an entirely grain-free diet, all his symptoms improved too. While we could interpret the situation he was presenting us in any number of ways, his main message didn't seem to be metaphoric at all, but point-blank instructions about my own diet—a good reminder never to overlook the obvious!

Once my health started to improve, nothing seemed to be quite as confusing as before. With increased mental clarity, I couldn't deny what had to be done. When I went home for Thanksgiving, I knew it would be the last that Aaron and I shared as a couple.

CHAPTER 18

I Meet the Future

Isak Denisen noted that perhaps God made the world round so that we wouldn't be able to see too far down the road. When I was a girl playing with sticker stars, I had no idea that I would grow up to be a woman with stars in her lineage. Or that mountains could fly through walls and speak to me. Or that wise old Chinese books could reliably help me navigate the world. Or that the time when things seemed scariest was precisely when I should jump in. But that's what I'd come to.

Roughly five years after that first tantalizing suggestion from the *I Ching*—that my wildest dreams would come true if I followed through on the notion to change my name—my life had utterly changed. I'd gone from being twitchy and fearful and shy to living more and more with loving compassion for myself and others. The schisms in my brain that caused me to discount whole octaves of experience had been healed. I'd awakened not only to the nature of my soul's path but also to connections vastly more expansive than I could ever have suspected. Miracles, I'd come to believe, could happen. Not only that, but they needed to happen if the world were going to transition to a more beautiful place.

My divorce from Aaron was as gentle as it could possibly be. We divvied up our stuff, made a plan for selling the house, and tried to figure out what might come next. After so much time weathering my grief with perfect calmness, Aaron took out our old photo albums one night and started crying over them. It was an emotional breakthrough that showed me that he would continue growing and changing, becoming more authentic, more open, more beautiful—and that we could still facilitate that for each other, albeit in a different way.

In the end, my longing for children was met in a very unexpected way. As part of my work with the Santa Fe Time Bank, I met Charles Eisenstein, author of *The Ascent of Humanity*—which had so impressed me some years earlier—and *Sacred Economics*. Two months after our first date, I moved in with him—and his three sons. My life went from utter ease, tranquility, and heartbreak to total chaos and a true heart connection practically overnight. My house is now full of kids—anywhere from one to twelve, depending on birthdays, sleepovers, play dates, teenage dramas, coordinating schedules. In addition to getting to cuddle, nurture, and simply be in the magnificent presence of three truly great kids, I also get woken up and barged in on and asked for things constantly. I am frequently overwhelmed by the massive change I've wrought in my life—and I wouldn't have it any other way. The womanly side of me is being seen and fully exercised. I'm no longer waiting for my life to begin.

For his part, Aaron still doesn't regret not having children. He never wavered in his dedication to his own path, and for that I am grateful—and more than a little ashamed that I tried so assiduously to change his mind.

In an email he sent after our divorce, he said this:

> I wish I'd seen things more clearly, found the course of action that felt right, and brought matters to the best resolution, one way or the other, sooner. In retrospect, I see that I became too passive.
>
> I wish I could have found the path that led to more love, more openness. 'Cause that's ultimately what I'm after. I suspect it's what we're both after.

Of course, as I type these words, I know we're both on our way to where we need to go, and feel grateful for the richness of our experiences and the still blooming feelings.

Our experiences together *were* rich and a part of me still grieves the connection we lost a piece of, but I've also come to see that the more we owned up to our essential natures, the more our fundamental incompatibility was revealed. We were like magnets amassing truth to ourselves—only to find out that, after that spiritual process, our polarities didn't meet up after all. We wish each other every happiness.

David Deida, whose books about the masculine and feminine interplay I recommend, said something pertinent to my situation in a recent podcast. Speaking about accomplishments, he noted that it's not so much that we grow from our accomplishments as we accomplish something, experience the disappointment of it not solving all our problems, and then grow from the obsolescence of the old idea. If I thought that stepping into a new relationship with a houseful of kids was going to answer everything, that idea was stripped away pretty rapidly, like, say, the first time one of Charles's kids asked me when I was going to leave, or when I realized that I was spending more time washing dishes and picking up toys than everything else combined, including sleeping.

In many ways, my new relationship is not so different than the one I shared with Aaron. Charles and I still have to dare to communicate, reach out when we're wounded, and make heroic efforts for each other all the time. We still have to work at it. But our hearts do seem to be able to find full expression together in a way that feels divine. I hope that Charles and I will have a child, but there's no way to say for sure whether or not we will be so blessed. Nevertheless, a long-standing contraction in my chest has finally eased—and that feels great.

The intimation from that first meditation in Peru—and from Eckhart Tolle—that we will be bringing about a New Earth has, for me, come to pass. I now live in a way that's radically different from many of those I see around me. When the oceans turn black and jobs disappear and bombs explode, I cry a little bit. And then I take a deep breath and trust that something amazing—something better than we could imagine—will emerge from the suffering if only I don't add to the mess by giving into any fears that arise from difficult events. In nearly every moment, I strive to be present to what is, to what my heart truly wants, to what seems like it would be the most fun, to love.

While my life—and every person's life out there—can be beautiful amidst the chaos, that isn't necessarily the fulfillment of the story. I believe that we have a collective power to shift the whole paradigm, to transform the heartache into a beautiful world built on love, trust, and compassion instead of fear, mistrust, and exclusion. We do this by relying on our intuition, believing in magic, and knowing that miracles are possible.

To get there, each of us needs to find the courage to leap, like Jumping Mouse, into the great river. The awakening process isn't always easy. Confronting our fears, facing the unknown, embracing love in preposterous situations, trusting—all of these require the hearts of lions and the souls of lambs. But as each one steps onto this path, it becomes that much easier for the next and the next and the next.

If the things that happened to me are possible, then *anything* is possible. Just think what our planet will look like once we all know for sure that miracles are within our grasp. We *can* clean up the oceans. We *can* hear the sound of children as the loudest noise in the world. We *can* work in ways that make our hearts sing. We *can* lay down fear and suspicion and hatred and rage and turn, instead, to unity, community, love, and trust, all without compromise. We *can* ask for and receive one hundred percent, all of us.

As for the ETs and guides that I sensed along my journey, I have no idea if you'll find them in yours. It's possible that my ideas about our origins, both individual and planetary, are an expression of my own psyche, or of the current collective unconscious, poised as it is at the edge of the Earth's capacity and therefore, perhaps, reaching out for help beyond our borders. Or perhaps ETs arise in our consciousness as we take those first steps along the path of healing precisely because it's time to extend beyond ourselves in a way that we never have before. As we step into new modes of perception, it's important to look not only to the skies but also to the mountains, the earth, the seas, the trees, and the animals. Our need to come together as a planet, beyond national—and formerly rational—distinctions is undeniable.

Ultimately, I do believe that other beings are out there waiting to help us—but that won't abnegate our responsibility to ourselves as humans and our paths and choices. It does seem to be key that we start taking care of ourselves first. We do this, as Dr. Peebles points out, by learning to love ourselves more, forgiving ourselves, and being gentle with ourselves. The rest will follow from there.